DANIEL WEBSTER SMYTHE has published more than 1,000 poems in 87 publications, including *The New Yorker, Harper's, Saturday Review,* and the New York *Times.* His books of poetry are *Steep Acres* (1941), *Only More Sure* (1945), *Brief Inheritance* (1946), and *Man in the Land* (1953). In 1940 he won the Annual Award of the Poetry Society of America, in 1948 the Idol Prize ($500) at Union College, and in 1961 the Leonora Speyer Award of the Poetry Society of America. He has given talks and readings at the Library of Congress, the Poetry Society of America, the Harvard Poetry Forum, and elsewhere.

Dr. Smythe received his M.A. and Ph.D. degrees in American Literature at the University of Pennsylvania. He began teaching at Skidmore College, and for the last nine years he has been at Bradley University, where he's presently an associate professor of English. He teaches Versification, American Literature, and 20th Century Poetry.

Prior to World War II, which he spent overseas with Patton's Third Army, he worked on a wild life sanctuary in upper New York State and farmed with his father in Plaistow, New Hampshire. After the war, he began his undergraduate work at Union College in Schenectady, New York. At the age of 12, Dan Smythe wrote an epic poem in ten books entitled, *Atlantis.* He was born in Brockton, Massachusetts, distantly descended on his mother's side from Daniel Webster.

ROBERT FROST SPEAKS

by DANIEL SMYTHE

TWAYNE PUBLISHERS, INC.
New York 3

Copyright © 1964 by Twayne Publishers

All rights reserved

Library of Congress Catalog Card Number: 64-25062

MANUFACTURED IN THE UNITED STATES OF AMERICA
BY THE HADDON CRAFTSMEN, INC., SCRANTON, PA.

FOR RUTH

"I talk in order to understand; I teach
in order to learn."

ROBERT FROST

Preface

THIS BOOK is motivated by a deeply-felt obligation to share with the multitude of Robert Frost's admirers and disciples knowledge which I alone possess. Suppressing any inclination to criticize, censor, or philosophize on the material offered, I simply have acted the role of recorder. Robert Frost speaks, and the reader may draw his own conclusions.

Although I had heard him lecture, I first met Mr. Frost in May of 1939; I saw him last on August 2, 1962, a few months before his death. In the space of those twenty-three years, my acquaintanceship was a source of rich experience, for Mr. Frost repeatedly invited me to his home and offered a friendship which I eagerly accepted.

I attended Mr. Frost's lectures in various parts of the country; I even learned shorthand to take down his words, intending some day to publish them, in hopes that more people could share the value I found in them. When invited to Mr. Frost's classes at Harvard, I recorded my impressions painstakingly. Later, when I talked with him in the quiet of his study, I made mental notes on everything he uttered; when I left him, I hurriedly recorded his words while they were fresh in my mind. I know these transcripts of conversations are more than reasonably accurate; I have a well-developed memory for the type of vivid talk Mr. Frost offered. As the late John Holmes said, ". . . half a dozen people spent what they knew was a good evening, and would say so even now, but if you asked them what was said, not one could tell a single thing. But you have saved the evening forever. You brought it all back, and

I found no errors. . . . These accounts of yours are most valuable."

Purposely, I have refrained from removing *all* sensitive material—that which might tend to offend someone—with no intention to insult but a clear obligation to show truthfully all sides of Robert Frost. If I have been the instrument of embarrassment to someone I regret it, but I hope that those who imagine themselves thus injured will be mollified by the knowledge that this great man even knew who they were. Not attempting to eulogize Mr. Frost or minimize his shortcomings, I present him as I knew him: a powerful personality with many of the weaknesses and failings common to all of us.

This book then is both a recording of a man's words and his portrait. The words speak for the man and of his impressions; they emphasize his ideas, his recollections of a rich life, his interests; they illustrate his style of conversation, and they pass on many of his favorite stories.

For permission to reprint excerpts of material from *Collected Poems*, I am greatly indebted to Henry Holt and Company. For suggestions, reminiscences, and encouragement in this work, I give my thanks to many people, including Lesley Frost, Lawrance Thompson, the late John Holmes, Charles Green of the Jones Library at Amherst, Alexander Taylor of the University of Connecticut, Henry and Lansing Christman, Kenneth Porter, Thomas P. Haviland and Sculley Bradley of the University of Pennsylvania, William Gillis and Olive B. White of Bradley University, Fred Lape, Kimball Flaccus, Frank P. Piskor, Vice President for Academic Affairs at Syracuse University, John Hall Wheelock of Scribner's, Gerald Brace, Raymond Holden, Lewis M. Woodruff, Anne M. Witmer, Paul Oehser, Wallace Fiske, Burnham Eaton, Charles Norman, Wilbert Snow, Louis Mertins, and Kathleen and Theodore Morrison of Harvard University.

DANIEL SMYTHE

Contents

Preface   9

Introduction   13

CHAPTER

    I. The Lecturer   27

   II. The Conversationalist   34

  III. After the Reception   44

  IV. At the House of Mr. Holmes   52

    V. On the Train with Mr. Frost   59

  VI. The Classroom   69

 VII. Mr. Frost at Home   77

VIII. The Visit During the War   88

  IX. Round Table in Washington   93

    X. Mr. Frost in Cambridge   102

  XI. A Visit and a Lecture   109

 XII. Robert Frost in Vermont—I   121

XIII. Robert Frost in Vermont—II   132

XIV. Robert Frost in Vermont—III   138

 XV. The Last Ripton Visits   145

Index   153

Introduction

ROBERT FROST was the greatest man I have ever known. His influence on me and my ideas has been so immeasurable that it is hard to imagine my life had I never known Mr. Frost and his works. Throughout more than a score of years, I had constant access to his thought, his understanding, his artistry and vision. I lived and enjoyed Robert Frost for so many years that he has become a part of me.

His place in the forefront of American poets is secure, for in him we have an abiding inheritance which grows stronger with the years. His individuality, his insight, his acute psychological interpretations, his integration and sincerity, the forceful vitality with which his poetry abounds—all combine to make him the outstanding poet of this century. The reader has only to turn to the astounding *Collected Works* to realize that we have in Mr. Frost a major poet to be ranked above the best in our literature.

In a remarkable demonstration of Yankee perseverance, Robert Frost developed his poetic genius by himself throughout a period of twenty unrecognized years. Until he was almost forty years old, his work was turned down by editors as being too "rough" and vigorous for their readers. It was not until he had gone to England in 1912 and had made an impression there with his first two books—*A Boy's Will* and

North of Boston—that his reputation began to grow on this side of the Atlantic.

When he returned to America, recognition of his great talent came almost immediately, and the years that followed the early twenties up to his death were a record of honors and publications. He won the Pulitzer Prize four times, the only poet so honored; and besides numerous honorary degrees, he won election to the American Academy of Arts and Letters, medals from literary societies everywhere, and special commendations from the United States Senate and House of Representatives. There were other honors too myriad to mention. Few poets have been so widely and extraordinarily acclaimed as Mr. Frost was in the last twenty years of his life.

Robert Frost gained some renown as a world traveler for the cause of poetry, venturing to South America, the Near East, the Soviet Union, and it is no exaggeration to say that he was the best-selling poet of this century, his total sales of books exceeding one million copies.

My fascination for Robert Frost began in my high school years. Until I happened upon Untermeyer's *Anthology of American Poetry* and became absorbed by the work of Sandburg, Masters, and Frost, I didn't know there was such a thing as modern poetry. Groping to find style and themes for my own writing in 19th century models, I had my ideas of poetic composition completely changed by these three poets. It was mainly Mr. Frost who jolted me out of that rut, but his appeal was so strong that I became slavishly imitative.

I spent my youth on a New Hampshire farm not far from Derry and Franconia where Mr. Frost once lived, so we both had similar backgrounds and interests. After high school I farmed with my father and devoted my spare time to studying poetry, and I discovered in Mr. Frost a poet who wrote about things I knew intimately: grindstones, apple-picking, haying, scythes, axe-helves, pasture springs, spring pools, hornets, barns; I recognized his striking New Hampshire characters; his background and pithy phrasing struck a familiar and responsive chord in my mind. I proceeded to read everything I could find of his, with delight and enthusiasm and the growing conviction that here was the greatest poet of our era. It never occurred to me that someday I would meet and converse with Mr. Frost.

Before entering into this discipleship I had been trying to write blank verse in the tradition of Tennyson, but I was never very comfortable with it. The blank verse of *North of Boston*, all new to me, astonished me with its flexibility and power, and I spent hours analyzing these "roughened" lines to discover the key to their success. Mr. Frost gave me a great deal of homework, but I have never regretted it.

In the midst of these years of poetry study, farming, and nature study (for I had a vague idea of becoming a naturalist instead of a farmer), purely by accident I came upon the notice of a little magazine on the lookout for nature poetry. Called *Trails* and published near Schenectady, New York, its editors were Fred Lape and Henry and Lansing Christman. I offered my poems and they were accepted. Later, Mr. Lape invited me to visit his place and the home of the Christman family, The Christman Wildlife Sanctuary. This was a turning point in my life and led indirectly back to Mr. Frost, for the poet knew the family.

Particularly drawn to the wildlife sanctuary, I stayed on when asked; for on those several hundred acres being returned to forest I found excellent opportunities for nature study and the writing of poetry. Moreover, I discovered an extremely congenial and interesting group of people, led by W. W. Christman, who in the latter years of his life was writing beautiful nature poetry. In other words, I found for the first time people who were sympathetic, understanding, interested in what I was interested in, and eager to help me. And Mr. Frost was no stranger to them.

Proceeding to divide my year, the greater part of it going

to the wildlife sanctuary and the rest to farming in New Hampshire, I did some work for the Christmans, but I also did a great deal of studying and writing. Long, free-wheeling discussions with the family resulted in a new education for me. It was through their influence and my continued preoccupation with Robert Frost's work that my own poetry improved to the extent that national magazines like *Harper's* and *Scribner's* were receptive to my work. Needless to say, the early poems showed the influence of Mr. Frost, but that apparently did not hurt them.

In these years, the mid-thirties, my writings attracted the attention of the Harvard Poetry Forum and John Holmes of Tufts College. This led eventually to my first hearing Mr. Frost on the lecture platform and then to meeting him. This was a delight I had never anticipated, for I thought it was enough to do my best as a farmer, an amateur naturalist, and an eager enthusiast of poetry.

Born in San Francisco, California, March 26, 1874, Robert Frost remained in the west for eleven years until his father died in April of 1885. Not a great deal can be said about this first decade of his life. He lived on Leavenworth Street. He was baptized into the Society of the New Jerusalem (Swedenborgian) by the Rev. John Doughty, who lived not far from him. He had a fairly happy time of it, roaming the hills around San Francisco and walking along the Pacific, or running errands for his father during his political campaigns. In a few later poems, he was to recall some significant memories of California.

His mother was Belle Moody, whom his father had met while both were teaching in a small Pennsylvania town. Harvard-graduate William Prescott Frost had been born in

Kingston, New Hampshire, and was the ninth generation of this New England family. In his brief life, he became a teacher, an editor, and a politician. The man was of a restless and independent nature, some of which certainly found expression in his son. He went west to get away from a New England that was smug and Republican. He was a Democrat and a firm believer in states' rights. During the Civil War he had shown his strong sympathy for the Southern cause, even going so far as to consider joining the Confederate Army. In San Francisco he worked on the Democratic San Francisco *Bulletin*, eventually becoming its editor. Politics appealed to him; he ran for tax collector and was defeated. He was a delegate to one Democratic National Convention, and he was manager of the Democratic City Committee when it backed Cleveland. When his son was born, he named him after the famous Southern general.

In this period of its history San Francisco was not a dull town to live in. It was a fast-growing and violent community. Danger shadowed the life of a newspaper editor in that city— but the father did not mind it. He did have poor health, however, and he eventually succumbed to tuberculosis while still in his thirties. He left his family destitute.

His death caused a drastic change in the family's fortunes. The boy and his sister were taken by the mother to 96 Tremont Street in Lawrence, Massachusetts, the home of his father's father. This grandfather was the overseer in a Lawrence mill, and he generously offered a home to his daughter-in-law and family. The boy went to the Lawrence schools for a number of years; his mother taught there. She had written verse and reviews for the San Francisco *Bulletin*, and she read Robert stories at night; but he did not take literature seriously himself until he was fourteen years old. About this time he discovered poetry, being drawn first to the work of Poe and then going on to Bryant, Keats, Milton, and Shakespeare. He tried his hand at rhyme, almost immediately. The first poem that we have record of, written when he was about fifteen, during his sophomore year, was published in his school paper. It was entitled, "Song of the Wave." We might expect this would be a very poor poem, as poetry goes. It began,

> Rolling, rolling o'er the deep
> Sunken treasures 'neath me sleep,
> As I shoreward slowly sweep.

It contained inversions, contractions, stilted language, obvious rhyming; but it also showed a rollicking spirit and some care in metrical scanning. It promised well for one so young.

He had other poems published during his school days, but it was not until he was nineteen that he received a check for a poem from *The Independent*. At Lawrence High School he met the girl who was later to become his wife. She was Elinor Miriam White. They were co-valedictorians of their graduating class.

When he got out of high school, he wanted to get married at once, but Elinor White's family were dubious about the match. They suggested that the couple get a more advanced education first. So Elinor went to St. Lawrence, where she eventually took her degree, and Robert went to Dartmouth. But college routine was particularly wearing upon him, and in a few months he was back home. When he returned, he found that his mother was having a difficult time with disciplining her pupils in her little school in Methuen. So he offered to take over the teaching chore for a while. His first act was to thrash the two biggest boys in school; after that neither he nor his mother had any trouble.

He was over eighteen now and still anxious to get married. When the girl's family continued to object, he could not persuade her to leave school, so he left home in disgust and became a tramp for a while. He was fond of telling about this unusual period in his life, and in a way, it reflected his characteristic determination. He wandered through the South and ran into all kinds of astonishing adventures.

When he finally got home, he went back to doing odd jobs. He worked in Lawrence, reported for a newspaper, edited a "column" of short sketches, and even tried story-writing. He tried to sell some of his poems, but all of them were rejected.

When he was nineteen, however, a check came from *The Independent*—and he told his grandfather he wanted to be a poet. His mother was very happy, but the grandfather was disturbed. He knew that one could not earn much money writing poetry, so he shrewdly suggested that the boy try it for a year and then get another job if it did not pay. Robert suggested that the grandfather give him twenty years instead of one. As it happened, it was almost twenty years later that his first book was published.

When he was twenty-one, in 1895, despite his failure to achieve anything concrete, Elinor White's family reluctantly consented to the marriage. They were married in a Swedenborgian Church, although her family were Universalists. For two years the couple existed in Lawrence with what odd jobs he could pick up. One of them was editing a weekly paper called *The Sentinel*, for a while. Finally, at the family's insistence, he went back to college to try to complete his education. This time he went to Harvard. For two years he kept up with the college classes, finding himself drawn to philosophy, Latin, and Greek. But in the end, he gave up again.

His disappointed grandfather gave him a house near Derry, New Hampshire, where he went to farming. He was not a good farmer. He milked the cow late so he would not have to get up early in the morning. But he stuck it out for about ten years—or roughly the period between 1899 and 1909. However, all was not farm work; beginning in 1906 he taught English and dramatics at Pinkerton Academy in Derry.

In describing this period on the farm, he spoke about his three hundred white Wyandottes, his preparation of them for market, and his work at various places on other farms. His work at Pinkerton Academy was not easy. He carried thirty-five hours of classes a week, more than any other teacher in the school. At one time, he was offered a job at the New Hampshire Normal School in Plymouth, but he turned it down.

In 1912 he took his wife and family to England. The choice of that country came through the flip of a coin; it was to be either Vancouver or England, and the latter won the toss. When he went abroad, he did so because he knew that living was cheap there; but this was not the only reason. He realized that recognition in his own country was not to come easily, and he decided that possibly a change in locale might help. He had the idea, moreover, of writing a novel and supporting himself entirely by his pen. With these ideas in mind he settled with his family in a little cottage in Beaconsfield, a town in Buckinghamshire. Later, when their savings began to dwindle, they moved to a farm in the West Midlands of Gloucestershire, the "Little Iddens" farm. Here he did some farming, raising just enough to feed the family and reduce the household expenses. This was in early 1914.

During the three years in England many significant events took place. First, Mr. Frost met several important poets including Lascelles Abercrombie, Wilfrid Gibson, Edward Thomas, and Ezra Pound. A few of his poems appeared in Harold Munro's magazine, *Poetry and Drama*. Two collections of poems, *A Boy's Will* and *North of Boston*, were accepted for publication. The acceptance of these came by a series of coincidences, as he was fond of telling his friends later. He was in London when he saw a notice in *The Times* that Harold Munro had arranged a meeting of poets in his Poetry Bookshop in Bloomsbury. Frost attended the meeting, met F. S. Flint in the crowd, and was assured that he should meet Ezra Pound. Pound advised him to send his manuscript to David Nutt. As it happened, Mr. Nutt had been recently drowned in the horsepond behind his establishment, but his widow was carrying on the business. She accepted his manuscript, *A Boy's Will;* and when it was published, Pound gave it its first review. Frost always contended that this strange chain of circumstances led to his fame.

America was in the midst of a literary revival at this time; and Robert Frost, as soon as he had won the approval of some of the leading English poets and critics, was discovered as one of the stars of this revival. He came back to America in 1915 for several reasons, the main ones being that his money was gone and the wartime atmosphere in England was uncomfortable. When he got off the boat in New York, he saw on a newsstand a copy of *The New Republic* with his name on the cover and the title of his poem, "The Death of the Hired Man." He was invited to give the Phi Beta Kappa poem at Tufts College; and at this reading the editor of the *Atlantic Monthly* invited him to contribute some poems to his magazine. The following year he was invited to be on the advisory board of the *Seven Arts Magazine.* He was elected to the National Institute of Arts and Letters. Soon, Harvard University invited him to give the Phi Beta Kappa poem there.

In 1916 Alexander Meiklejohn offered Frost a position at Amherst as a full Professor of English. This was quite unusual, since he did not have a degree. But this stroke of luck came about again by a coincidence. A man by the name of Stark Young happened to read *North of Boston* and was quite impressed by the poem, "The Generations of Men."All the characters in the poem belonged to the Stark family of New Hampshire, of which Mr. Young was a member. Mr. Young was also a member of the Board of Trustees of Amherst College, and he used his influence to have Mr. Frost invited there to teach.

The American edition of *North of Boston* had been published by Henry Holt and Company in March of 1915. One month later, they brought out *A Boy's Will*.

Amherst was very good to him. Classes were few, and he was able to devote a great deal of his time to poetry. In 1921 the University of Michigan asked him to come out as "poet in residence." He went back to Amherst in 1923. In 1925 and 1926 he was again at Michigan. All this time he was writing his books, spending his vacations in Vermont, helping to found the Bread Loaf Summer School, and assisting in the production of a play he had written, *A Way Out*.

After his two-year stay in Michigan, he remained in Amherst from 1926 to 1936. In 1925 he bought a farm in South Shaftsbury, Vermont; later he bought other places nearby.

The period from 1928 to 1934 was remarkable in that he had no work published in national magazines. Such a lacuna in his publications may have been due to sickness and death in the family. Also, he was having some trouble with the administration at Amherst, which eventually resulted in the "clean break" of 1936. But in spite of family troubles, he was still receiving honors and still publishing books. In 1928 he had published *West-Running Brook* and the second edition of his *Selected Poems*. In 1930 his first *Collected Poems* came out, and he was elected to the American Academy of Arts and Letters on November 13. In 1931 he won the Pulitzer Prize for poetry for the *Collected Poems*. In 1931 there also appeared a new edition of *A Boy's Will* and a third edition of *Selected Poems*.

1936 was a momentous year, not only for the break with Amherst but because he was made the Charles Eliot Norton Professor for poetry at Harvard. His published work included *A Further Range*, which became a Book-of-the-Month selection. In addition, his *Selected Poems* was published in London, with an introduction by himself.

In 1938 his wife died. Of all the deaths in his family, this was the most crushing blow. (One of his daughters, Marjorie, had died in childbed fever; and a little boy, Eliot, had died at four years.) He was so stricken by the death of his wife that he neglected his health and had a serious spell of illness. All his life he had felt that she was the greater poet, and he had relied upon her criticism of his newest poetry. He used to say that sometimes he would get her "mad" so she would give him valuable words straight from the shoulder. She was very sensitive to criticism herself, and when his work received an adverse review, his first thought was of how she would take it. She worried about her children. She was hard-working, and Frost, in the early years, had given her little help with the housework and the family. But that was all perfectly satisfactory with her. She had great confidence in his genius and wanted him to write while she took care of the home.

In 1938 and 1939 he delivered the White Lectures in Lawrence, Massachusetts. This series was paid for from a fund set aside to perpetuate the memory of a noted citizen of the community—and Frost was given this opportunity through the efforts of enthusiastic admirers in that city. He was elected to the Board of Overseers at Harvard in 1938, and the following year was given the Ralph Waldo Emerson Fellowship of Poetry there.

During the war, 1941 to 1945, he published several books, including *A Witness Tree* (for which he received the Pulitzer Prize) in 1942, and *A Masque of Reason* in 1945. In the late forties, he followed these with three more books, *Steeple Bush, A Masque of Mercy*, and his latest *Complete Poems*. In 1941 he established a scholarship at Middlebury College in memory of his wife.

Indeed, the remaining years of his life are remarkable for his activity, the honors showered upon him, his reading tours, and his travels to foreign lands. He said that what he wanted to do for the rest of his life was to "consolidate our position" in American Literature.

His travels led him to Sao Paulo, Brazil, in 1954, where he

was a delegate to the International Writers' Congress. In 1957 he went to England, where he received honorary degrees from Oxford and Cambridge. Still other trips were made to Israel and Russia, where more honors were given him.

In 1958 he was appointed Consultant in Poetry to the Library of Congress, and later he was given a new appointment as Congressional Library Consultant in the Humanities. The Congress of the United States offered two Resolutions in 1950 and 1959; and he was delighted to do so when asked to read a poem at the Inauguration of President Kennedy.

In 1962 his last book, *In the Clearing*, was published. He died on January 29, 1963.

When thinking of Mr. Frost, I remember his energy, his congeniality and friendliness, his endless round of stories and ideas, his stubborn independence, and I think of the terrific impact of his poetry. I often wonder why he was so friendly and cordial to me, why he spoke so intimately to me of his personal affairs, why he took me into his confidence. Perhaps part of it was my New Hampshire background and that I was a young and struggling poet without much formal education; in other words, I was someone such as he had been. Perhaps, too, that was why he kept urging "independence" upon me. "Go it your own way. You will be better for it," he wrote in a letter. This is more clearly seen in the following incident: I once had occasion to ask him for a statement about my own work for publicity purposes, but he refused me, strongly, urging that I should not turn from a "dreamer into a schemer." He felt I should keep my independence; he admired it in me.

Robert Frost Speaks

CHAPTER I

The Lecturer

HARVARD UNIVERSITY with its elms, its famous Yard, its Widener Library, and the thousand-and-one memories of its past surrounded us; I found myself in one of its lecture halls, awaiting the words of Robert Frost. I was seated on the floor in the middle of an aisle, and wedges of people were banked on my left and right, in back and in front. They sat on the radiators, in every aisle, and they lined the four walls. Even the edge of the speaker's platform was hidden beneath students, who dangled their legs and looked out over the audience. This hedge of humanity grew restless as time went on. I had planned to fill a notebook with what I heard and saw, but the crowded conditions interfered with that.

It was to be my first glimpse of Robert Frost, and the time was a late March evening in 1936. To be sure of a seat, I had arrived a half-hour before he was scheduled to speak, and I was lucky to gain even a tiny spot on the smooth floor. Only the people in the seats were comfortable. Many of us willingly had to endure discomfort, but this spoke well of the drawing power of this singular personality.

When Mr. Frost appeared at one of the entrances, he seemed surprised and a little moved at the sight of so many people. I heard him mutter (he was not far from me), "Oh, you shouldn't have done it . . . you shouldn't have done it!" Then he moved straight forward through the mass of people to the lecture platform.

He was a short, stocky man, but I felt at once that here was a man with an immense spread. He was the center of the audience, and no one could mistake his strength and confidence. As he shouldered his way along, he seemed purposefully intent. (Years later, he was to say to me, "See the way clear, and then go plowing ahead!") His large grizzled head moved among these people and put down a trail of hush as he passed. As soon as he gained the platform, he stared at the closed book in front of him. Then he looked up with a smile as the heavy applause began to subside. From where I sat, I could see that his hair was very white and thin, his face square and strong, and there was a continual half-smile around the lips. From the start, he seemed at home with his audience.

I wrestled out my notebook and pencil and prepared to make a stenographic report of every word uttered. I put down the initial sentence: "In my first talk, I praised being lost to something that gives you direction—and direction is the great thing." At this point, someone hit my elbow; another person coughed into my ear. I gave up. I decided to concentrate upon what he was saying and how he was saying it. Also, I would make some mental notes about the personality of the speaker. But in the midst of such a large audience, even that was not easy.

It took me a little while to get accustomed to Mr. Frost's style of speaking. He used no notes whatever. Before he got warmed up to his talk, he hesitated a great deal, groped for the right word, lost the thread of his sentences, and rambled away from what he was talking about. I got the immediate impression that he was the poorest speaker I had ever heard; a literal transcription of what was said would be a mixture of unnecessary words, unfinished sentences, and even ungrammatical constructions. It took me but a short time to change my mind.

I noted immediately that the audience was enjoying him immensely, and he was well aware of it. The pleasure he derived from speaking spread out into every corner of the hall. With every gesture of his powerful body, he radiated friendliness and understanding and confidence. I was vividly impressed by his sturdiness and his belief in what he said. And I felt a measure of that confidence and joy in the faces of the audience around me.

His manner of talking changed a bit as he went on. He evened out his sentences and kept to his subject. His mind was a huge field of ideas, and in this field he struck associations here and there. But he had a central idea to begin with, an idea he had mulled over before the lecture. And everything he said shaped itself around that idea.

I found that some of his ideas stuck in my memory like burrs. (While he was speaking, I forgot my physical discomfort.) "Performance means conformance," he said. "A poem is an adventure," he added. "The poet lives his adventure." With some of his dry, humorous remarks he was able to keep a straight face, but he was not able to suppress the twinkle around his eyes.

After the lecture, he read some of his poems—"Mending Wall," "Birches," "The Runaway," among them. He enjoyed it when his audience insisted on more; one felt he wanted them to like his poems. "I don't want to keep you," he said, "but I will give you one more." And then he gave us several more in the midst of a deep silence unbelievable for such a large group.

This first experience of hearing Robert Frost gave me a lot to think about. I desperately wanted to get one of his lectures down on paper, to see what it would look like. I was to take down many of his lectures in later years, and its difficulty was immediately apparent. His lectures were not satisfactory pieces of prose; the transcriber often found it necessary to do a little work to aid the "sense" of the piece. To show what I mean, here is a word-for-word paragraph from a lecture, "The Anthology as the highest form of Criticism," I took down in Lawrence, Massachusetts.

"We will sort of play with an anthology I have contracted to make: but as I think I told you back a while, you can contract to write all books you please and nobody can make you write them. That is one of the nice things about contracts. Whenever you are thoroughly ready. I have contracted to make an anthology in my old age. We would have to go to law to determine what old age is. Then it would have to be proved, I suppose, by the party of the other part that I had not a weak head and so could make an anthology if I wanted. I have approached it in various ways. I spoke of the anthology as the highest form of criticism. People disparage anthologists when they speak of anthologies—anthologists as people who reap what they haven't sown. Two anthologists, Jessie Rittenhouse,* now all the time in Florida, Louis Untermeyer, they make a great deal of living out of poetry. Lots of people around like the little boy I used to know. He wanted to sell an old jackknife or something. 'What will you take for it?' 'Five cents.' 'Oh, you want to make money!' People think anybody who wants to make something is a capitalist. I never was that way about anthologists. And I suppose I have profited by them more than they have."

I have heard Mr. Frost termed a "slovenly" speaker. It is true that his hesitating and groping for words made it difficult to record his lectures, but I was not the only one to attempt to take him down. Whenever I could find his printed lectures, all of them struck me as having been corrected and smoothed out. I was to learn eventually that Mr. Frost did not like his words recorded: perhaps the thought that some sentences

* (1869-1948) American poet and anthologist.

might be incoherent caused him to object. There were others who felt this. At one time the president of a national poetry society objected strenuously when I offered one of Mr. Frost's lectures for the club's bulletin.

In the course of time, I learned to straighten out his sentences as he spoke. I did it automatically. But I had to be alert every instant and work with the greatest rapidity. As an example of this kind of transcription, I would like to quote a paragraph which I took down at Tufts College in Medford, Massachusetts. This is not word-for-word as he spoke them, but the "sense" is one-hundred-percent accurate.

"I was trying to think whether this was the same room that I read three poems in about twenty-one years ago. I don't remember the room—I was too scared. But I remember the three poems. These three appeared in the *Atlantic Monthly*, all together. They were taken away from me, to my amazement, by the editor. The reading of them *here* led to the editor taking them and asking for them. I had reached a point of pride where I had to be asked. Such were the relations between him and me. Those poems did a load of good. Then there was this: there came along with the poems an article that fell out of the sky. You should charge this happening being luck—not merit. The editor wanted to know what I had been up to. He said, 'Have you got somebody in England to write articles about you?' He said, 'Do you know Edward Garnett?' I said, 'I have never met him.' He said, 'He has written an article about you, but I have not decided to publish it.' I said, 'If you don't publish that article, I will tell everybody in America.' And so the article and the three poems came out together."

The fact that he was a "rambling" talker became clear in all his lectures and conversations. When he began a lecture ("If the Anthologist Includes His own Writing") in Lawrence, Massachusetts, he tried mightily to keep to the subject at hand

—the anthology. But in spite of his efforts, he was led away by other ideas. After beginning with a summary of the most popular anthologies, he started to speak of education and schools and someone he met on a train in Oklahoma. He wrenched himself away from the man who was "telling such a truth as that," and suddenly said, "Now take the anthologies." After going along smoothly again about "thoroughness" and methods of teaching, he was side-tracked to the college verse that was being published and the fashion of teaching writing. But he finally snapped himself off with, "But we must keep to the anthology. . . ." A few sentences further on, he was off on the subject of judging poems for a school magazine, and then he brought up the story of how some people were gossiping around about a "quarrel" between himself and Archibald MacLeish. He enjoyed telling that.

When it came to the reading of his poems, he rambled still more. For example, after his lecture on anthologies, he said he was going to read "Birches," but he began by going into the background of the poem, the inspiration of it, and much of the correspondence surrounding it. Before he got to the poem itself, he had given us a list of his favorite poems. Finally, he remembered that he was to read "Birches," and he picked it up and started to read.

Any one of his lectures might be called an adventure in rambling. He had a mind full of information, convictions, memories, ideas—and a lecture was simply a dipping into these. He might have a subject to dwell upon, but he found it exceedingly difficult to keep himself to that subject. This way of lecturing, however, seemed very satisfactory to most of his audience.

This can be borne out by what happened after that first Harvard lecture. Working myself free of the crowds of people, I joined a small group headed for a lunchroom and a discussion of the evening over a cup of coffee. There were many opinions voiced in the late hours of that night, and every word concerned Mr. Frost. I remember one excited student who vowed he realized what the poet was up to, and envied him. He brooded over the thought for a long time, and finally burst out with, "Why, that man is like a ten-year-old child. He does just as he damn pleases!"

CHAPTER *II*

The Conversationalist

THREE YEARS after Mr. Frost's lecture at Harvard, on an early May evening in 1939, I was given the opportunity of actually meeting and talking with the poet. John Holmes, of the Tufts College faculty and a friend of Mr. Frost, had promised to arrange this after I had expressed eagerness for an introduction. A letter had come from Mr. Holmes inviting me to Tufts College, and I had gratefully accepted. Mr. Frost was to be on hand at some exercises of the Phi Beta Kappa Society, although the poet was to be Raymond Holden.*

When I arrived at Mr. Holmes' residence in Medford, the Phi Beta Kappa poet and his son, Dick, a student at Harvard, were already there. Mr. Holden, a distinguished poet, unassuming, boyish, talkative, welcomed me very warmly. He carried his cap and gown for the occasion.

We walked uphill onto the Tufts College Campus, and I was talking to Dick about his college studies when we saw Robert Frost strolling toward us. I now had my closest view of him. He still had that faint smile around the eyes, the white uncut hair, the faraway look as he stared across the campus. With his rugged, thickset body and square face, he seemed the strongest of the group. He welcomed us with as few words as possible since he was almost out of breath from

* (1893-   ) Poet, novelist, and biographer of Lincoln.

[*34*]

climbing the hill. When Mr. Holden, as a joke, asked him if he had just walked from Boston (eight miles away), he said quickly, "No, but I could do it." I had heard before of his restlessness and his endurance in walking long distances. He wanted us to know that his walking ability had not decreased.

As the five of us walked about the campus, he astonished me by moving a pace ahead and beckoning me to walk with him. He seemed to take a sudden interest in me.

"Where was it you said you lived?"

"In Plaistow, New Hampshire."

"Oh, yes, we called that 'out back.' What do you do? Do you teach?"

"No. I do farm work. Gardening."

"What kind of a farm do you have? How many acres?"

"A vegetable and poultry farm. We have about thirty-eight."

"Have you always lived in Plaistow?"

"No, I was born in Brockton. Before Plaistow, I lived in Atkinson, New Hampshire."

"You have? I know Atkinson. Used to know a man named Hall* from that town, a very fine man. I knew him for years and years. Do you know that many parts of your section (parts of Derry, Atkinson, Chester, Hampstead) used to be a part of Massachusetts? Did you know that?"

I had to confess I did not. I wondered how far back in history that was, but I was too shy to offer the question. However, he was not through with me.

"Are you going to college?"

"No, I'm not. Not right now."

"That's good. You would have to be careful of what college might do to you. I'll have to tell you about college sometime. I ran away from it when I was young, you know. You have some things published?"

---

* Mentioned in the poem "New Hampshire" as coming from Windham, but Mr. Frost had taken poetic license with his birthplace.

"A few."

"Are you preparing a book?"

"I am putting one together."

"What is the title of your book?"

"*Steep Acres.*"

"Are your acres steep?"

"Not very steep. But we do have a few hills and slopes."

"Well, I should know that! How about this farm of yours? Are you devoted exclusively to gardening?"

"Not entirely. It's a chicken farm."

"What kind of chickens do you have?"

"New Hampshire Reds. Also, we have a garden and woodlot."

"A lot of trees on the place? Any apple trees?"

"We have a small apple orchard."

"Do you spray your trees?"

"Some years we do, but not always."

"Do you raise apples to sell? Or do you just use them for pies and applesauce?"

"Mostly applesauce."

"Are you married?"

"No, I'm not."

"You live then at home? You and your father run the farm, is that it?"

"Yes."

"Do you often come to Boston?"

"Only once in a great while."

"Well, we'll have to get together sometime when you are in Boston. I want to have another talk with you. I'm glad I saw you here tonight."

We turned back to the others and continued our stroll until it was time for Mr. Holden to dress. Several things interested me. The two poets talked almost constantly, and the rest of us were content to listen. We met a number of people on campus to whom Mr. Frost was introduced, and I was attentive to their reactions when the name of the poet was offered. A Professor Lewis, a stout, oldish, bearded man, said when he was presented, "How do you do, Sir. I know you very well—not in the flesh perhaps, but through your books with which I am well acquainted." Mr. Frost bowed and smiled. Another man we met was a divinity student who said, "Mr. Frost, I have used your poem, 'Birches' in one of my sermons." The older man brightened up at this and exchanged several words with the student in regard to the sermon. I found myself thinking that everywhere the poet went, the same shower of compliments must have been heaped upon him. People's faces would change at the mention of his name, and they would search swiftly for some happy compliment to say on the spur of the moment. I wondered if this constant rain of compliments was a bother or a source of secret satisfaction to the one upon whose head it fell.

In the course of the conversation he showed an apparent dislike of colleges. Several times, he made ironic remarks about them. Even when Holmes took us all out front to see the splendid view of Boston, he was not cheered to any great extent. He mused, "It must be a nice place late at night when everybody is asleep." Later, I heard him state emphatically, "There are no letters at a college."

We attended the exercises, Mr. Frost listening with half-closed eyes to both Holden and the orator of the occasion, a scientist. His reaction to the latter was evident in what he said to Dick later: "What the scientist said was nothing: it was unimportant. The only thing there was the poetry." And when we walked down the hill, it was apparent that the scientist's ideas were festering, for he suddenly burst out with, "He was holding out on us. Why didn't he tell us something about his special line of study? All he offered was high school science. He refused to let himself go." A few steps further, he spoke again, "These fellows think it is so easy to solve anything; they have everything planned out. What he gave us we all know. What interested me most was the little crystal that separated the voices in a single telephone wire; I would have liked to have heard more about that."

As we passed the football field and turned the corner of the street, I heard Mr. Frost begin to chuckle. He said, "You know, these fellows who fight so strongly for peace—and peace. Sometime they will win out, and we'll have peace everywhere. But what will happen? Some day, when all the men are sitting around crocheting, one of them will get up and say, 'Oh, I'm sick of this. I want to do something different. I want to start trouble.' And he goes ahead and does it. Then the whole thing starts all over again."

In Mr. Holmes' library, the first topic of conversation was Edgar Allan Poe. Mr. Frost said he used to like him very much; he quoted several lines which he knew by heart. Among them were these:

And the mist upon the hill
Shadowy—shadowy—yet unbroken,
Is a symbol and a token—
How it hangs upon the trees,
A mystery of mysteries.

But he disclaimed any great admiration for Poe now. "Three or four things," he said. "Good things—but the others, no." Mr. Holden recalled a line from the "Haunted Palace." The line consisted of one word, "Phophyrogene." Mr. Frost recalled the two lines that had excited Swinburne a great deal:

Whose wreathed friezes intertwine
The viol, the violet and the vine.

From Poe, he went to a story he had recently heard. It concerned a man who had joined the Episcopal Church and was about to make his first confession. A bishop of the church was his confessor. The fellow insisted, "I haven't anything to confess. I haven't done anything wrong that I can remember."

The bishop said, "Well, can't you recall a single thing? Haven't you ever sworn, or...."

"Oh, yes," said the man. "Come to think of it, I remember once I swore. It was in my college days and during a football game. We were in the last quarter, the last minute of play, and I was the quarterback. The score was seven to six against us. We were close to the goal line, and I called my signal to take the ball over. The play started, and I plunged through the side of the line and over the goal. But then I suddenly found that I did not have the ball. And I thought fiercely to myself, 'Where in hell is that ball?' "

At that moment, the bishop perked up and said, "Where in hell was it?"

Everyone laughed heartily over this.

An important item of conversation was an article which had recently appeared in a leading magazine. Someone had interviewed Mr. Frost, and the poet had not dared to read the result. The interviewer had been no friend of his, and he had hunted him down in Philadelphia to demand that certain questions be answered. It was hard for us to imagine Mr. Frost's being chased around the city—as he wanted us to assume that he had—but he drew a good picture of his tormentor and repeated some of the questions.

"Now we are going to get to the bottom of this: what is the guiding hand behind your verse?" (He avoided answering this.)

"Whom did you mean in 'The Lovely Shall Be Choosers' by 'she'?"

Take twenty years.
She would refuse love safe with wealth and honor!
The lovely shall be choosers, shall they?

Mr. Frost's reply was that the woman he meant was his mother—this was rather disappointing to the questioner! Throughout the interview, he tried to sheer away from the personal—from references to his wife—but in this case he was goaded. "The fellow," said Mr. Frost, "was out to get me. I knew he would hurt me in some way if he could."

But he *had* granted the interview—so he had to endure the painful, perspiring business. Just why the man was so antagonistic was not made clear—but he was! "In your poem 'Reluctance,' he had said, "you have just teased and flouted. You are a teaser and a flouter!" When the poet tried to explain that a poem began in delight and ended in wisdom, the retort was that his (Mr. Frost's) began in knowledge and ended in perplexity.

The difficult interview finally came to an end, and the published article was around somewhere, but he had not read it. His secretary reported it was not as bad as expected. I must admit I had the feeling throughout this long account that the poet was not quite as persecuted as he made out, that he would be a match for anyone of that type.

He mentioned Ann Winslow, a lady poet and editor who had conducted a contest for college poets. "I didn't want to be a judge in this contest, but she insisted. She wouldn't take 'no' for an answer. There were about three hundred poems submitted. She had selected about a hundred. Every now and then, while reading them, I would throw the whole bunch across the room against the wall, and my secretary would gather them up, and I would go at them again. She had not arranged them in alphabetical order. I guessed she had put them in the order of what she she thought was best—so finally, I gave first prize to the first one on the list and split second prize between two and three. It is possible she put the bad ones first, and the best ones last."

He went on to tell of the impression he gained from reading the poems. To him all the poems seemed to have been in one style of writing—as if one teacher had told all the poets a single way to write.

Speaking of this editor reminded him of what else she had once done for him. They met at a writers' conference in Colorado, and when he told her he was suffering from the high altitude, she gave him some pills that were supposed to help. He carried them around for a while and showed them to everybody at the conference. One pill could lower the elevation 1,000 feet. But he never took any. He threw them under the bed.

Mr. Frost relished telling about episodes in his life— these episodes generally involved other people. When Mr. Holden mentioned MacLeish, the name prompted Mr. Frost to tell his favorite story, the account of their famous quarrel. When they were together at the conference in Colorado, they had a long discussion about a certain part of a poem, "The Air Raid." Mr. Frost did not believe that women would run out and wave their skirts at attacking bombers to make them cease. Moreover, he did not believe there was any instance of such a happening, in the Spanish or any other war. MacLeish admitted that the idea came out of his imagination, but he thought it might easily have happened. That was their disagreement—and their friends had made it into a "quarrel."

They talked of Cale Young Rice, a Kentucky author who recently had written Mr. Frost. A line that had irked him was, "I am glad that you for one have been able to eke some recognition out of the public." He implied that he had been unable to, although he deserved recognition just as much as the other. He was one, said Mr. Frost, who had battled hard against the Chicago magazine *Poetry*, and he was the author of a terrible line of verse:

Clad, ah, in her bright sarong.

In connection with novel-writing, Mr. Frost said, "Literature is being written too easily, today." He cited Bernard DeVoto, a friend of his and an editor on the staff of the *Saturday Review*, as an example. This man had just finished his second twenty-thousand-word novel and was much disturbed because Mr. Frost could not find words of praise for it. The praise went to his earlier work—and that did not please this "successful" author. "He is writing tripe," said Mr. Frost. "He had one of his slipshod stories in *Collier's*. I tried to read it, but I couldn't stand it."

Speaking of people in general, he said there were two kinds of people he liked: the ones who just do not give a darn about anything but go ahead and work; and the ones who just succeed, accomplish things. The type he especially disliked is the fellow who keeps saying not *mea culpa* but *tua culpa* and *sua culpa*. Another type is the one who continually rails against the times and his lack of success because of the badness of the times, the implication being that if he had been born in any other time, he would have been able to do wonders.

During the course of the evening, he spoke a little on religion. He said that Professor Lewis had spoken of Tufts as "a school of religions" instead of the school of the Universalist denomination. And Mr. Frost agreed that this was what Universalism meant: it took in everything, as it should.

"Religion hasn't given up the fight yet," he mused, "not by a long shot. And there is always some new religion popping up. I know a man who joined a cult whose habit it was to jump up in the air and bang their heads against what they thought was a trapdoor so that the 'Great Light could get through to them.' He vowed that he himself was not very religious; in fact, he committed ten sins a day. When Mr. Holden contended that this was an impossibility, he said, "Already you don't give me credit for originality."

When he was asked what faith he had been baptized in, he

said he had been in several denominations before ending up with the Swedenborgians, who had baptized him thoroughly. He was much amused in telling the story of a friend who, when he made out his college record, put in after "faith," "Anti-Episcopalian."

The talk went on until long after midnight, with Mr. Frost as animated at the end as at the beginning. He was thoroughly enjoying himself, repeating stories, describing episodes in his past, and recounting humorous incidents at the expense of his friends. His final contention was an argument in favor of the twentieth century. Too many people were acting as if nothing really bad had happened in the world previous to now. They complained against the horrors that were taking place, as if they were peculiar to the present. In reality, this century was much better than other centuries. One had only to look into the history books to see that.

He prepared to leave with this parting shot. He shook hands warmly with all of us and said that such an evening would bear repeating. When he went out of the door with that half-smile still on his face, I saw him go with some regret. This had been the best evening of talk I had ever had.

CHAPTER III

After the Reception

O N AN EVENING in late May of 1939, I was invited to Tufts College again. Mr. Holmes, impressed by my attentiveness at the last visit, had resolved to have me meet Mr. Frost again at the first opportunity. This came sooner than anticipated, for Mr. Frost was to give a lecture; there was to be a reception afterwards, and then an evening of talk.

Everything went very well. I attended the lecture and struggled through the reception. Later, to my amazement, I found myself wedged into a car with several faculty members of Tufts College—and Robert Frost. We were bound for Cambridge and a place called the Hotel Commander.

I counted this a lucky stroke. Despite the exultant tumult in my mind, I became determined to collect as much as possible in the way of conversation, impressions of Mr. Frost himself, and his exact words. I drove from my mind all thoughts of the others in the party. I tried not to clutter up my thoughts with their appearances or what they said. Every available space was to be loaded up with Robert Frost.

It seems I kept my eyes on him the whole evening. I saw a thickset, seemingly very muscular, not-very-tall man with white hair that looked as if it had not been combed that day and needed cutting: in the back, it overlapped his collar. There was a humorous twinkle playing about his eyes most of the time, but he talked sometimes with his eyes almost completely closed, leaning forward on the table. Especially when he was describing the events of his youth, he seemed to be studying a mind-picture of the road he walked. Having listened to many discussions, I have found that some of the most talkative people are too busy framing new pearls of wisdom to listen carefully to what others are saying. But I noted Mr. Frost never once made the mistake of not listening to what all the others said. That is, he never pushed a different train of thought over what they were saying, even though he did more talking than the four of us put together.

As he sat there, he toyed with a couple of spoons. He seemed to be enjoying the people and the courses of all our minds. I noted that he wore a plain gold ring on the smallest finger of his left hand and that these hands were covered rather heavily with hair. The skin of his face was weather-beaten and brown; there was a wart on his left eyelid. He did not show his teeth as he talked, and he had a heavy lower lip denoting stubbornness, I believe. He had a delightful, impish laugh which he was not chary of. There were quite a few wrinkles around his eyes, and there were lines in his forehead, which had a bulge in it. He had a short, snub nose, a strong chin, and a quizzical, dreamy expression about the face that is hard to describe. His appearance was firm and set; he was solid there at the head of the table. I must say, also, that he had a gentle, interesting tone of voice, and when he looked at a person, his gaze was a pleasant one.

He seemed anxious to talk on every conceivable subject. The first thing discussed at the table was the new five dollar edition of his *Collected Poems*. Mr. Frost said he liked the spine, but not the design on the cover; that is, the design was all right, but he did not like where they put it. Not only that but the cut by Lankes* was of his son's home and not his own. Seemingly, his publishers never knew this. Mr. Lankes

* Illustrator of Robert Frost's books.

was paid ten dollars for the cut, and it had been used four times for this book. "So you see," said Mr. Frost, "why he is gnashing his teeth out there in the Middle West, while we are sitting here so comfortably and having such a good time."

He said many people had been worrying about him. One in particular, Hervey Allen* (who made all his money on one book), had been instrumental in getting him to go to Cuba last winter. Hervey thought he should "brace up, snap out of it, get to doing something." So he arranged with Paul Engle** and his wife that Mr. Frost should go to Cuba.

Mr. Frost reported that he was not greatly impressed by the country. Havana was just a mock Paris, a poor imitation. Every bus in the land drove like fury, loaded with poor people going nowhere very fast. If a bus is a minute late, the driver is fired; consequently, they drive madly, and Mr. Frost glimpsed the worst wreck he ever saw anywhere. (He drove by just after it happened.)

Apparently, they were known by no one in Cuba, for there were no brass bands to meet them, not a soul to direct them. The only one to mention poetry was the houseboy at the hotel who, on seeing Robert Frost, held up one hand dramatically and declaimed:

> It was many and many a year ago,
> In a kingdom by the sea,
> That a maiden there lived whom you may know
> By the name of Annabel Lee.

And he added, "I know you. You're a poet."

Their chauffeur was a "dirty fellow" who lived in a hovel outside of town. He had been to school in Pennsylvania and in the American navy, so he considered himself a full-fledged American. He had a great deal of native intelligence, and Paul Engle pumped him dry. Engle was one of those young men, a Rhodes Scholar ("whom I am going to see in a few weeks at

---

* (1889-1949) Author of *Anthony Adverse*.
** (1908-   ) Iowa poet and teacher.

his home in Iowa"), who had an active mind and a great curiosity. He learned everything about the country and the language from this chauffeur in not a long time. Weeks before I had learned from Mr. Holmes that Mr. Frost wasted little of his time reading long books. But he did want to know about them, so he gained his knowledge by asking questions about a book to get firsthand reactions. It was evident that he tried to keep himself aware of his former close friends over the country by asking every conceivable question about them of anyone who had contacted them recently. Thus, when I mentioned a man named Charles Malam, a Vermont writer, a former Rhodes Scholar, and a good friend of Mr. Frost about the time Malam left college, I was instantly deluged with quick questions.

The name made him turn on me like a flash—as I suspected it might: "Where is he now? . . . What does he do for a living? . . . Is he married? . . . What does his wife do? . . . She probably earns more money than he does, doesn't she? . . . Is he writing? . . . What does he want to do? . . . Does his wife teach in a college in the city? . . . Has he any children? . . . How old is his child?"

These and many other questions he fired at me like a machine gun, his eyes suddenly sparkling with interest.

During the evening at the Hotel Commander, he seemed to take a delight in insisting that places, mountains, lakes, forests —everything that was regarded universally as worth visiting for scenic beauty—had no interest whatever for him, in spite of the fact that he was one of the most-traveled of poets. People held him. Nothing else mattered. This had been a lifetime habit.

"I do a lot of traveling but I never pay much attention to places. I don't go anywhere to look at things. I am not interested in lakes and mountains and lands. When I was in Cuba, I didn't try to look for anything. When I was in London, I didn't have any desire to see a thing in the whole city. Let me tell you a little story. I made two visits to a friend in Gloucester, England. On the first visit, I had to walk up and down for some time, waiting until he was ready to see me. Ten years later, I went to see him again; and I found myself once more on the very same spot, walking up and down, waiting for him. Then I suddenly discovered that I was standing in front of the Gloucester Cathedral. It occurred to me that instead of walking up and down, I might as well drop in and look around as there was supposed to be a lot of history attached to it. I did. I walked around, looked at shrines and things. Then I went to see my friend. Ten years before, I hadn't noticed the cathedral."

One faculty member, Dr. Harold H. Blanchard, had made a literary study of the whole of England; the thought of disregarding historical and literary shrines must have been appalling. I enjoyed this bit of conversation:

Dr. Blanchard: "You lived near Oxford?"

Mr. Frost: "Yes, lived almost next door to it."

Dr. Blanchard: "Did you ever go over to visit it?"

Mr. Frost: "Nope. Never bothered about it once."

I wish I could reproduce the tone of relish and satisfaction with which he made this last statement. He was actually proud of his indifference.

He liked to ramble in his talk from subject to subject, and the conversation was steered around to the South. Mr. Frost recalled that when he was about nineteen years old he became a tramp, not caring what happened to him. This is how he went on:

"I had one dollar in my pocket when I found myself in North Carolina. I walked and walked. I came to a river (here his eyes were closed and he seemed to be back there) on which there was a boat. I asked the captain how far he would take me for a dollar, and he designated a certain place. So I

[*48*]

got aboard, took my place on the boat after inquiring if there was any work for me. The first thing I noted was that it was loaded up with jugs and jugs of whiskey. Most of the men on board were hunters, and whiskey was a part of the business. That evening was a lively one—one of the liveliest I had encountered—because everybody on board became drunk except myself and the captain. Men were lying around on the floor everywhere. And one man had a violent spell of delirium tremens. Someone threw a bag over his head. It was an awful, screaming, violent night.

"Leaving the boat, I wandered on—and into lumber camps. Terrible places. Plenty of liquor and work and badness. Great big strapping Negroes. Every night, there would be fights in which blood flowed freely. Adventures galore.

"I kept wandering—through desolate country. The natives doing nothing, but lined up, holding up the stonewalls. Cotton was five cents a pound: terrible low price. It was in the midst of a bad depression. Bad conditions. . . . Once I was walking through a swamp. The only thing that kept me above the mud was a board walk extending for miles. Right behind me strode a stranger, a giant Negro with an axe on his shoulder. He followed my heels for three miles. At any moment, he might have hit me on the head and pushed me off into the swamp and no one would have known anything about it. That was a scary experience.

"I happened to meet someone there—someone who worked in a girls' academy. I met the head of the place, had a fairly good time for a while. But I had not a cent in my pocket. So one day, I walked off without anyone knowing it.

"Finally I got back to Baltimore."

Unfortunately I have to do without the quirks of facial expression, the individual style of talking, his laugh interposed here and there, and his vivid touches in describing places on his route.

He began to ramble off again when he spoke about his classes at Amherst:

"In those early years, three classes a week were enough for me. Even that seemed quite a lot. I gave lectures on philosophy and reading. When I stop to think of it, only two people of any importance came out of those classes. One was Joseph Monchure March, the author of the *Wild Party*. But this fellow has now given up writing altogether and has gone over to Hollywood. The other pupil was E. Merrill Root.* My conscience bothers me because I have not answered the last two or three of his letters. Recently there has come a pathetic letter. Root said he would like to send on his latest book but he wasn't sure that I was interested anymore. I must attend to this. I will do better now. In the old days, I formed a habit of putting all unanswered mail into a large box until I should have the time to answer them. But when the box was filled, it was always a temptation to start a new box. Letters all the time—and sometimes from the most patient of letter-writers. And autograph-hunters. Continually people send me my books through the mail without enclosing return postage. They think I can well afford to do this. Why do they do it? A common sort of letter in the mail is this: Someone will write and say, 'I have a chance to appear in book-form if I advance a certain sum of money to the publisher. Shall I do it, Mr. Frost?' My answer is always this: 'If you feel there is a need for it, that you have to have these books to pass around among your friends and relatives so that they may think well of you, if you need something to bolster you up, then go ahead and send the money.' As for me, I have pride. I would never do it in my life. If it had happened that my books would have required such a bargain with a publisher, they would never have been published. They would not be known today if that were the case. Pride won't let me. But I suppose one must have recognition, however. One must get around.

* (1895-   ) Poet and author of *Shoulder the Sky*.

[*50*]

Too often deserving poets do not get around and undeserving poets do. Nancy Byrd Turner is a fine poet, writes wonderful stuff. A good poet that says a great deal and deserves more than she has received. On the other hand, there's Angela Morgan. Awful! Nothing worth considering. And yet she gets around."

The rest of the evening was spent in talk on a wide variety of subjects. When finally we started to leave, it was close to one-thirty in the morning. In the lobby of the hotel, I followed Mr. Frost as he paced nervously back and forth in the corridor. (We were waiting for the taxi.) I casually mentioned that bluebirds, meadowlarks, and purple finches had returned early this year to New England—as early as March. He exclaimed, "As early as that!" He asked me again where I lived; when I spoke of Plaistow, New Hampshire, he said, "Oh, yes. I remember that you told me. I have been through that section very often."

We took Robert Frost to his apartment. When he got out, he shook hands with everyone. He appeared pleased with the evening we had given him, and there was an affectionate note in his tone of voice when he bade us good-bye. As he walked into the hall of his house, I saw him look to see if there had been any mail. That was my last picture of him that night— felt jacket, rubbers, quizzical expression still on his face.

CHAPTER IV

At the House of Mr. Holmes

ABOUT A YEAR LATER (March of 1940), I had the opportunity to see Mr. Frost again at the home of John Holmes. I had received an invitation from the latter to come to Boston, and this I accepted with alacrity. Mr. Frost happened to be in a gossipy mood on this particular night. He was fond of talking about people anyway, pro and con; his stories occasionally had something of the caustic in them. He had no respect for certain personalities, and he did not hesitate to state his beliefs or to repeat a story he had heard about someone.

He seemed to look younger than he had the previous year. He was active and talkative. He did not mention our previous meetings. I conjectured that in the interim he must have met and talked with more people than I would see in a lifetime. He had traveled far and had lectured and taught. An evening of conversation and reading such as we were about to have must have been a common happening for him.

Someone had called his attention to a review of his work by Louise Bogan in a leading magazine of the day. Mr. Frost said he was positive she had never read any of his work, at least no more than one poem. Years and years ago, she had come to the conclusion that that particular year had produced but one poem of merit. The poem was Mr. Frost's "Fire and Ice."

Now in this review, she had recalled that poem. And she went on to say that he did not treat the cities kindly. Mr. Frost, a little heatedly, said that only once had he ever put the city into his poetry: his one and only "Freudian poem," "A Brook in the City." In this poem, he had mentioned a "repressed brook." The dear lady had read this and nothing more.

Someone asked if his first teaching job was at Pinkerton Academy. He said, "no." He had taught country schools when he was eighteen. He added that he had tried his hand at almost everything. "And I have never done an honest day's work in my life, if I could get out of it." The reason he taught school at such an early age was that his mother had been taken ill, and he was recalled from school to take her place in a little country school. He remembered that his first job was to lick the two biggest boys who had been a source of constant worry to his mother.

Mr. Frost, comfortably seated in the best chair in Mr. Holmes' sitting room, enjoyed the friendly regard that all the company had for him. He sipped at a glass of ginger ale and talked. Ginger ale was his favorite beverage, and I watched him drink three glasses during the evening. But the adverse review was still rankling, and before long he returned to it again. This episode was an example of his extraordinary sensitivity to criticism. I was to be reminded later of this when I talked with Archibald MacLeish about the poet. Mr. MacLeish said, "His reaction to criticism is a surprising thing to me. Frost is like a rock in our literature. Nothing can disturb his place. And yet, if some of the younger people berate him, he gets disturbed. I recall that recently there was an adverse review or something, and Frost ripped the writer to pieces and in public. There was no need for this. He should have ignored it."

To keep Mr. Frost in good spirits, the company tried to steer him away from this unpleasant subject. Someone brought up young children's writing poetry and asked what he thought of that.

"I wouldn't advise a parent to send out their work or try to sell it. Don't make too much fuss about it. It's so apt to fade out then. It's sort of a cursed memory to them. They remember having been thought something of once and having lost it completely.

"At two or three, when a child is first coming into the world, he has a gift that poets can envy. It's a way, using words in ways you never saw before. A new use of words. This is one of the great things in poetry. We have never tried that before, yet it can be done. Using words, loosening them. The baby does that and makes you laugh for a little while. The child surprises.

"This goes on from three to seven years; then it seems to go away. Then what they have is just a singsong speech. That is in a way all right if we don't make too much of it. That phase is going to fade—but he could hold it over like a change of voice, if it is not noticed too much. Let it develop.

"Edna Millay appeared young in *St. Nicholas*. So I don't know what to say about it. I do think the child is to be encouraged. I would never encourage a child too much in school. It is just the same with other things."

Mr. Frost's last visit to Tufts College was recalled. Someone remembered that he had been the Phi Beta Kappa poet there about twenty-five years earlier and that there had been a small report in the college paper which read, "Some interesting poems were rendered by Robert Frost, the poet." The orator of the occasion, however, received several columns. Mr. Frost spoke of his reading that evening. "I went through them so fast they all seemed one." A little while before that he had sent the three poems to the *Atlantic Monthly* and had had them returned with the acid comment: "We have no room for your vigorous verse." But right after the reading at Tufts, the editor accosted him and said he must have those poems right then and there. Mr. Frost handed them over. They were the same ones that had been handed back to him as "no good" by that magazine. But now the *Atlantic* went ahead and published them a couple of months later, no one on the staff saying a word. In due course of time, he told the editor about it.

Mr. Holmes spoke of Van Wyck Brooks, who had praised a book which no one liked. This recalled to Mr. Frost a visit and an argument he once had with Brooks. The latter had a strong-willed wife, a woman with vigorous political ideas that Van Wyck followed meekly. But on the porch, when he was alone with him, Mr. Frost said, "I bullied him. I got him to admit that it wasn't happiness that we were after. Just as long as we had the work and were in a fair way of accomplishing it, that was all that was needed." When they went into the house, Mrs. Brooks burst out with, "Mr. Frost, isn't it wonderful that we're doing our utmost for the happiness of the human race!" Robert Frost told her rather gleefully that her husband had just admitted that happiness did not amount to a damn: it was only work that counted. She glared at her spouse. "You said that?" she said.

On Holmes' sitting-room table, he noted a copy of the *Atlantic*, and he thumbed through this for a few minutes. It reminded him of his early troubles with the *Atlantic*—and he found little to say in praise of the poems he saw in these pages.

He read us some poems, and pretending we were a larger audience said the things he customarily said before each one. He began, "About 'Birches' I usually say something like this: 'I have a poem I will read you tonight, and it is about birches. It is about swinging birches. I saw somebody down in Ipswich —somebody who knew who I was—with other young people. They got past us and got ahead and began to swing birches, straight up, and when they got to the top, they threw themselves forward and got down to the ground head first. We didn't do it that way.'

"Then out west, some lady sent word to the place where I was reading, she wouldn't be there that night. She wouldn't come to listen to a person who could tell such a story about a birch tree. She had one in her yard, and she knew very well it would break if anyone did do a thing like that, and that I didn't know what I was talking about.

"About 'Pasture' I usually say this, in this style: 'I will lead off with one that is taken more often by the anthologists than any other. It is one somebody used years ago to express something I have been talking about lately—how we have talked on the subject of "Confusion." "In these confused times," everybody says. Everybody has an opinion of "these terrible times." I notice Dorothy Thompson did. This one was used long ago, when I was young, to express the opposite of confusion. The first stanza is called unclouded.'

"Did I tell you about the confusion, the game of confusion I played the last time I was out west? Somebody said to me (he was a lawyer): 'I am confused. I am really confused.' I said, 'In the medical sense?' You see I felt obliged to do something about it, so I said, 'Let us play confusion.' 'How do you do that?' he asked. I simply say, 'Are you confused?' and then you ask me if I'm confused. I said, 'Now, are you confused?' 'Yes, I said so before.' To me, he said, 'Are you confused?' My answer: 'No. I win.'

"I have always had an interest in that word, 'confusion.' I don't think I really thought of it in this poem, but it could be thought of in connection with it. I wrote it a long time ago. I never had a greater pleasure than on coming on a neglected spring in a pasture in the woods. We clean out the leaves, then wait by to watch the uncloudiness displace the cloudiness. That is always a pleasure to me; it might be taken as a figure of speech. It is my place to see clarity come out of talk and confusion. You didn't need to know that was in the poem. But now you see that was the way it was used."

Bringing out the poem "Dust of Snow," he said, "Here's one, a little one, used often in the anthologies. It is all one sentence, two little stanzas. I have called it 'the favor.' I often feel a special favor to find a flower I have not seen for a long while, or hear a strange bird I haven't heard in years.

"Once sitting in the kitchen in the last of a sunset, a great owl darkened the room. For a minute in the last sunlight, he showed the whole underside—the quills clear. The sight of that bird right close to you is just like a favor, something you did not expect—as if someone was on your side. It is like that often in the newspaper. You see something that pleases you. Some team that won or something like that. I used to say that I had a feeling of changed luck if I read in the morning paper that both New York teams had lost doubleheaders, because I grew up wanting Boston to win. In the far west, I began to take sides with Chicago because I lived in San Francisco— long ways away. It's the same way with nature. You feel flattered when something is vouchsafed you like that."

He next read an old favorite, "Stopping By Woods on a Snowy Evening."

"This is one that gets into the anthologies more than any other. The greatest danger is that your mind will get too busy over a poem. You don't have to get busy at all—just let it alone. On the whole, it's kind of fun. You don't go to the circus to make a lot of discussion—you go to gape. There is nothing hard in that poem, but there is a busy-mindedness that makes people want to know about a little thing like that. What is there to know about it? Somebody wants to know what his name was. Will the woods really fill up? That is the way they treat it. Then they write, 'Who was that going home that way at night?' Their teacher puts them up to it. I wonder if there is anything more to it than just wanting to know. They hope you will get excited and write them a letter. Someone asked me if a horse could ask questions:

> He gave his harness bells a shake
> To ask if there is some mistake.

'Can a horse ask questions?' I was asked that. It was a professor asked it, and it was in a horsey country. All I had to do was to turn to the rest of the people. There was Frank Dobie* who was born on a horse, I guess. I looked at him. (He wears one of those hats). I said, 'Can a horse ask questions?' 'Yes,' he said. 'A horse can ask questions, better questions than some professors.' "

On this evening he said in connection with the poems that most of them were portraits of persons. "A poem is always a portrait. That is the important thing." It was one of the most impressive things I had heard from him.

On this visit, as on all my visits with him, I found him brimming over with anecdotes. At his mind's tip were the many experiences, impressions, and ideas of a rich life. He seemed to revel in imparting everything. Each single poem had a long chain of circumstances connected with the writing of it. I shall always remember the way he radiated the thoughts of his large life, as well as his boundless good humor. He had much to give, and I, for one, was eager to receive.

---

* (1888-1964) American writer and collector of Western folklore.

CHAPTER *V*

On the Train with Mr. Frost

ROBERT FROST'S SON, Carol, committed suicide on October 8, 1940. On the day after, quite by accident, I rode on the train to Vermont with the bereaved father. Many months had gone by since I had seen him at the home of John Holmes. On this particular afternoon, my destination was Albany, New York. I had taken a place on one of the cars of the Berkshire Limited in Boston and was looking forward to a colorful trip across Massachusetts. Train activity was at a high pitch—passengers taking their seats, buzzing conversations, streams of people passing the window, engines panting on nearby tracks. Suddenly, across all this activity, one man projected himself; and I sat upright in some excitement. A burly man came shouldering through the aisle, followed by a slight woman in grey. He seemed in a hurry to find a seat, or something, and walked the whole length of the car and back again. He finally sat down in a seat across the aisle.

He talked industriously for some minutes with the woman, then made a feverish search for a timetable. I leaned over and gave him two. As he took them, he thanked me, turned around to me again and managed a good hard look. "I've seen you before," he said. I stood up, smiling, and said, "At Mr. Holmes' place." He smiled, "Oh yes, Daniel Smythe." He introduced me to Mrs. Theodore Morrison, his secretary, who bowed and smiled and said that she also remembered my name very well.

I studied the woman carefully, having heard a great deal about her from Mr. Holmes. She looked about forty—a slight, pretty woman dressed in a grey coat and a grey sweater. There was a dark blue ribbon around her blue hat. She had a pleasing voice and an engaging smile and manner. I felt she would be a fine person to know.

Mr. Frost was a great deal changed from my last memory of him. His face appeared very tired, and there were new lines in it. He betrayed darkness under the eyes, and sometimes he talked in a faltering voice, particularly in the latter part of the trip. His hair was just as ragged and uncut. He had shaved, but it had been only a halfhearted job: there was an uneven patch of whiskers under his lower lip. He used a direct gaze but with eyes that appeared somewhat strained and unwell. He slouched wearily in his seat, seemed at times half-asleep back on the cushions.

He said he was now on his way to Vermont and that some people were going to meet him in Williamstown. Mrs. Morrison was going to leave the train at Springfield and return to Boston. That was the cause of all the fuss about timetables. I noted that he wore wrinkled, black, comfortable-looking shoes. The suit he had on was not very new. The quizzical expression had changed to a pained look. There was not a great deal of humor in his face: the odd, half-serious look was gone, as was the half-smile that used to twitch around the corners of his mouth. But in spite of all this, he was the firmest man on the train. Evidently he had taken a lot of battering in the last few months. When his hulking form went down the aisle, I saw the people turn to look at him with interest. One woman watched and whispered about him. I saw him try to look at the newspapers on his lap—the New York *Herald-*

Tribune and the Boston *Globe.* But he could hardly see beyond the front pages. His hands fumbled with a pair of horn-rimmed glasses in an old case. He did not use them. The train rapped and roared. Occasionally the secretary and Mr. Frost would display a show of interest in the town they would be passing through. (Valley Bridge, for instance.) They spoke its name. I do not think they once looked at the scenery or commented on it.

I came back after a short time, when there was a lull in the conversation. We touched upon Paul Engle. I asked them what he was like, and they told me he was a frail-looking man, thin but athletic. He had taken part in sports. He was not energetic or a great talker. On the contrary, he was rather shy, but very observant of people. He was not a bit like his *American Song* with its sweeping statements, wideness, tremendous reaches. He had toned himself down a bit. "Something has happened to him," said Mr. Frost, musingly. I asked Mrs. Morrison how she liked Engle's wife, and I received a quick smile from her. "Very much," she said. I gathered they had both seen the Engles last spring.

Mr. Frost leaned further back, looked at me with his brooding eyes, and talked. He talked about Hervey Allen, and Robinson Jeffers, and the "wave of patriotism" that was now sweeping the country. I noted again that he did not stare out the windows; or if he did, apparently he did not see any of the brilliant countryside. When we were riding through the highest hills of the Berkshires, strewn with color, he took no note. The forest was at its best, but it did not matter. (I remembered a previous talk in which he had stressed his unawareness. What we said and thought was more important, it seemed, than all the flashing pictures of the woods.) He pressed deeper into the cushions and words began to flow from him:

"Ever try the *Atlantic* with poetry?"

"Yes," I said. "I had some notes from Mildred Boie."*

Mr. Frost answered that she'd left the magazine. "She wasn't always to be praised for her selections. But it's hard to be good in selecting. It's hard to be true in writing." I mentioned that I thought it was Sir Philip Sidney who said, "Good poetry always tells the truth." "That's a good one. To a certain extent, 'yes.' We will always have to qualify that. It makes us fall back on the stock phrase, 'What is truth?' Age-old. Most of us only get to near-truths—and luck at that—in poetry. Now take Keats' famous 'Beauty is truth and truth is beauty, that is all ye know on earth and all ye need to know.' A fine beautiful-sounding phrase as far as it goes. It's an emphasizing statement with a rhythm to it. But we know well that truth is not always beautiful. Ugliness is truth. We must remember that."

Just before Springfield was reached, I went back to my seat. Mr. Frost dictated a letter to his secretary—something that was giving him a lot of bother. The word "depression" was an important word in it, for he pondered its value. When we finally drew into Springfield, he hustled Mrs. Morrison out of the car and into the station. While he was gone, I heard a Negro porter and a woman conversing about him. The woman claimed she recognized him and considered him the best of contemporary poets. But the porter thought he was rather "simple"—the way he was bustling around the station outside.

Very soon, Mr. Frost came back and took his seat beside me.

With his first words (and they were startling ones), I realized that I was seeing him at a critical time.

He said, "My son, Carol, died last night! He killed himself."

His own statement seemed to affect him very much, and ignoring my expression of sympathy, he urged me not to talk

* Poet and one-time editor with the *Atlantic Monthly*.

to him any more. I said I would not. I decided he was not distrustful of me; he merely wanted to rest. But despite his request for quiet, he did not really want it; for he talked almost incessantly on many subjects. I let him do the talking. He gradually perked up through the trip, seemed to respect me for my quietness. I liked it when he said, "There is a great deal to be said from the shy ones."

He spoke for a few minutes about his son, his life and what he was like. He said the man was very sensitive, and he had been a frail person, never in good health. He had written some poetry, but without any firm measure of success. His apple farm in Vermont had been his source of income.

After a while he turned away from this subject as if anxious to think of something else. He asked me about my poetry and then started speaking of the value of poetry, what a poet should do in building a poem. He said a poem should have a point—build a framework of beauty. It should be of fine texture. He pointed out poems in the anthologies which were quite perfect, as if made from sheer good cloth of a fine workmanship. A poet must write simply of what he knows . . . "like this man, Christman,* and his nature poems." He observed these things, thought about them, wrote on them. Too many of the would-be writers had nothing to write about: they could not put themselves, their feelings in the writing. Many parts went to make up a poem—the beautiful flow of the lines, the good rhyming, the leading to a point, the simplicity of the words, the truth of the whole idea. Most people lacked the ability to say what they mean. A good poet must have an *insight* into things—little bits of psychological understanding of a mind. Poets must turn out good fabric.

He said he had carefully arranged his first book—it was composed of lyrics—and just as carefully, he had worked on his second, a book of narratives. Both books had been written

* W. W. Christman (1866-1937) Friend of Robert Frost, poet, and owner of the Christman Wildlife Sanctuary, Delanson, N.Y. See introduction.

over a span of twenty years, but he had selected poems that seemed to tie themselves together. They seemed to build up like a single poem. The ending of *A Boy's Will* was the return to the simple things of the universe. Again, in *New Hampshire*, he had taken a single long poem; the other poems in the volume were sort of notes attached to it. All were related to each other. Yet, at the time of the writing, he had not thought of that. He did not believe in writing for a book. The title had much to do with it. It was his opinion that a good title attracted the editor's eye. On the other hand, he had been led astray on one book—*Mountain Interval*. He had been urged to publish it. It was just a bunch of poems slapped together, not judged and weighed like the previous volumes. What was the result? The book was his least successful; it did not sell very much. He had had it published with misgivings (giving in to the arguments of his editor, who was swayed by the success of the previous books); and it had turned out badly.

Speaking of *Mountain Interval* reminded him that once a man had tried to get even with him on it. Mr. Frost had refused to get this fellow a job or something—and he had written to Mr. Frost later that the book was an "interval" of going downhill. It was a lapse. A great many people had misunderstood the title. It meant an "intervale"—a bit of low land between high hills, an expression used by country people around. As an example of an interval, he waved his hand at the Berkshires in the distance.

We returned no more to the subject of his son's death. As I watched him talking on and on almost fiercely, I had the impression that he was striving to drive his thoughts in new directions. His sorrow was close at hand, but he must have known it would return with full force when he greeted his little grandson at Williamstown. He began to ask questions:

"Do you write reviews?"

When I said I had written only two, he said, "You are two

ahead of me. I have never done one in my life. Reviewing is a sad business. They can twist you all out of shape. Take Bill Snow,* who came down to see me the other day. One of the things that brought him was a review by a New York lady reviewer which was not very complimentary. In one of her sentences, she intimates that he could be more understood if he wanted to. In other words he had joined the ranks of the unintelligible poets. That's nonsense. I have seen his first book as well as his last, and there is no marked difference in their intelligibility. That shows you what reviews are worth."

I told him I had at home two reviews given John Keats—including the one in the *Quarterly Review* that discouraged him so much.

"You have? I have heard of them but I never read them. Is the *Quarterly's* review as bad as they say it is?"

"Yes. The most bitter words I have ever read."

"Are you able to quote any of those words?"

"As near as I can remember, the opening of the review of *Endymion* goes like this: 'Sometimes reviewers are accused of not reading the books they criticize. We honestly confess that we have not read this. We have not been able to struggle beyond the first of the four books.'"

"And then I suppose they went ahead and criticized the whole work. Think of reviewing like that! Do you remember any other part of it?"

"Well, they criticized his rhymes—ridiculed them. They sneered at the structure of his lines. They accused him of being a copyist, of being unintelligible and tiresome. They quoted lines to show what he did to 'our heroic couplets.' They tore his technique to ribbons."

Mr. Frost pointed out that "*Endymion* is an immature work, but it shows great promise. He did make mistakes, of course, but what did they expect? You can forgive him so easily when you go on to his next, *Lamia*, and the other

* Wilbert Snow (1884-   ) Maine poet and good friend of Robert Frost.

[65]

poems that are perfect. One can't do much better than 'Ode to Autumn,' 'Ode to Melancholy,' and the like. The reviews bear out what I just said. I wonder how near they came to killing him?"

"I don't think they did. You might be interested to know that a certain poetry magazine sends books to a certain critic when they want them torn to pieces. I met the reviewer, and he told me he believed that."

"What poets did he review?"

"The reviews I saw were of Robert Coffin,* Robert Hillyer,** and Merrill Moore.*** He had little to say in favor of any of them."

"They are not too bad. Let us take each of them. Take Robert Coffin. Some of his stuff is good. He's an easygoing poet, and he wouldn't make people rise up in arms. But he has good lines. I don't see why people belabor him so. Look through his book and you find a poem here and there.

"You said Hillyer? He used to be one of my boys. I first met him in 1917, I think. He presented me with one of his little books when I lectured at Harvard. I liked it. The man doesn't write extraordinary stuff, but it is good and competent. I certainly believe him to be the best of the academic poets. Well, he should be; he has the best chair in the college, one of the best in the country.

"What was the other? Merrill Moore? But his poems are just extemporaneous exercises. Strange but interesting pieces. An active mind spilling over—swift and unrevised. The reviewer should have taken them as curiosities—not poetry."

He asked me if I had been helped by Bread Loaf or the MacDowell Colony, of if any college had had me. I said,

* Robert P. Tristram Coffin (1892-1955) Maine author, friend of Robert Frost, and 1936 Pulitzer Prize winner in poetry.
** (1895-1962) Former head of the English department at Harvard and 1934 Pulitzer Prize winner in poetry.
*** (1903-1957) Boston psychiatrist and author of over fifty-thousand sonnets.

"no." "You are like me," he said. "I went at the whole business alone. I don't know why they do it. When a poet gets going, he will usually attach himself to a university, grab a professorship, and bury himself in conservativism."

Mr. Frost said that when he was younger, he had taken many voyages of discovery; he had investigated bogs and swamps, walked the woods. He had made discoveries here and there. One of the best was happening upon a little cave and finding it lined with a rare moss. It was strangely alight and had the color of green gold. It seemed to glow. This was so amazing that he stuck in his hand and pulled some away; at least he thought he did, but nothing came out in his hand—no light. He learned later that it was one of the rarest mosses that did this. On another occasion, he had found a rare violet. Still another time he had picked up some huge ladyslippers. Certain localities thrived with different kinds of plants. Didn't I find it so? Was there not a marked difference between southern New Hampshire flora and eastern New York state? He inquired about my sanctuary work and I told him about the thirty-three kinds of ferns that lined the fern trail.

When he had made his home in Salem, New Hampshire, he did a great deal of "discovering" there—walking for miles along the country roads and over the fields. They had a little house in that town. As he had often said in his lectures, most of his poems were written in a ten mile radius of Lawrence.

I asked him about his classes at Harvard, and he complained that this year it was a little mixed up. There were about sixty in the class when there should be about twelve. With so large a class, it was impossible to talk to all of them—and a great many wished for more time, wanting to talk over their problems with him.

When we reached Williamstown, he jumped up. He said it had been fine—this meeting me again and talking so much. He shook me warmly by the hand, bade me good-bye and good luck, and hurried away. Outside I saw a boy hurrying over to him. Without a word, Mr. Frost threw down his bag and put his arms around the boy.

I had met him on the edge of one of his greatest sorrows. His son was gone. But, as he said, "It's all in the way of the world," and pointing to a newspaper picture of a bomb-hit bus, "They were probably all killed. There are more sadnesses than mine."

CHAPTER VI

The Classroom

I N THE WINTER following the Lawrence lectures, I was invited to attend Mr. Frost's class in poetry at Harvard. Knowing I would not be able to attend many of the classes because of the distance I had to travel, I keenly anticipated the first view of Mr. Frost among his students. Upon my arrival in Cambridge, December 17, 1940, I feverishly combed the university for Adams House. It was a little disturbing to be at a loss as to its whereabouts. Boston streets had always baffled me; Cambridge streets were worse. (I had called up his secretary and learned that Adams House was not even on the college grounds.) Finally, going down a certain street, wondering which was the right house, I approached a stocky, bundled-to-the-ears figure. He had an old shabby felt hat on his head; an ancient light-grey coat hugged his form. His hands were buried in his pockets. He slouched close to the buildings, seeming almost ominous. Getting closer, I saw that it was Robert Frost.

He shook hands, showed me where the place was, and told me I had better go in quickly and grab a seat. He would be in later. I entered the Common Room and stood amazed at the unusual classroom. Every seat was taken by about sixty students who sat around tables, in corners, in rows in the middle of the room, and up against the walls. I brought in a chair from outside and was lost in their midst. Some of them were smoking; only a couple had notebooks. One was sitting on the floor; others were sprawled out in their chairs. The majority were talking quietly.

In front, directly before a large wood-filled fireplace, stood an old armchair. When Mr. Frost came in, he went directly to this chair and slid down into it. He slid down so far that he seemed to be almost outstretched before us. During the four hours that followed he hunched lower, never appearing to change his position. He became a part of the old chair. The shoulders of his wrinkled suit drew up until they were almost level with his ears.

I looked carefully over the room in which we were seated. It was not at all pretentious. The ceiling was unpainted. The walls were green with massive pillars at several-foot intervals on all sides. There was a huge table in the middle of the room and smaller ones in the corners. But it was the fireplace that caught the eye. It was very large, full of logs with no kindling under them, and dominated by a mantlepiece on which there was a bust of some famous man. Draped around the mantlepiece and the fireplace were wreaths of evergreen.

So Mr. Frost sat there, seeming to blend in with the whole setting. For several minutes he did not do anything, and occasionally a student would approach him with a book of poems. He would autograph each quickly and turn back to his musing. He had folded his coat on the floor beside the fireplace and had placed his hat upon it. The students still talked and smoked.

Mr. Frost seemed to be gathering himself for the forward thrust. I did not realize that he was to talk for more than four hours continuously—two and one half hours of the class and an hour and a half with some of his students after class.

For almost two hours I kept up with him in my shorthand notes; he talked slowly, hesitatingly, so there was no difficulty. I was captivated by the expressions on his face and his interest in the students. He seemed to be right at home and enjoying himself thoroughly. Occasionally he would slip in a profane or slang word, and once he used "ain't." He looked healthier and stronger than when I had last seen him in Lawrence. He smiled a great deal, wrinkled up his nose in disgust at certain poems, waved his hand in the air when he wished to denote birds and words going up into the atmosphere. He smiled and chuckled and changed his voice—made little side quips and often joshed his audience. In all the lectures I had heard from him, I had not seen him quite so good-natured, so lively in his talk.

Apparently he had picked up a few magazines that had come in; those were to be the lesson. He wanted to talk about certain poets of today who were rated as the obscure type. As usual, he beat all about the subject, delving into Shelley, the meaning of words, Lewis (the Labor leader), the ideal and the practical, "vested interests," the radical magazines.

The students listened to him with the greatest respect. They laughed heartily over some of the strange poems he read to them, and I knew he was glad they laughed. There was only one who muttered. He disagreed with Mr. Frost several times on his estimation of the poems, but he did not disagree very loudly. Mr. Frost never heard him. Once I heard him (he was right behind me) say, "On and on and on"—this after about two hours of talk.

After he dismissed the class, he made no move. When I saw several students drawing up their chairs around him, I stayed, too. This was the usual thing. He autographed more volumes and commenced to talk. It was good talk, full of the most interesting bits of information, wisdom, and wit.

He began by talking about Willa Cather,* his meeting with her, and his seeing her and General Pershing talking very

* (1876-1947) American novelist, short story writer, and 1922 Pulitzer Prize winner.

cordially at a party. It was a sort of reunion for them because the general had been her school teacher years before. She was a stern person, very set in her ideas, not much interested in the common crowd. Her new novel was being reviewed. It was about a Virginia family—and Mr. Frost could see what she had done. She had investigated Virginia "somewhat."

Mr. Frost said that all his life he had been careful not to investigate things and then write about them. (Bobby Burns had done that.) Mr. Frost wrote about what he knew. Amy Lowell* was a person who on several occasions made mistakes; she had written about work she did not know, for instance, shingling a roof. She had a carpenter shingling it from the roof (ridgepole) down. On another occasion, she had the shavings from a plane curving backwards instead of forward. "I wouldn't write a poem about a sewing machine, because I don't know anything about it."

He said also that he would not write about a Packard car because he was not sure the Packard would be here forever. For a time, he had worried about using "horse" in his poems, but he guessed that animal was due to stay. He liked to use the good, lasting words. He would hate to think that his poems in years to come would need notes of explanation on outmoded words. He had once wondered about "snow," had asked a New Orleans audience pointblank if they knew what snow was. The majority of them had some idea; they had seen scatterings of it here and there, in the mountains perhaps.

He did not consider himself a New England poet, he said, although he had had many people tell him they enjoyed his poetry so much because it brought back to them the New England touch. He had lived in a great many places. He did not find people much different from various localities anywhere.

I thought I detected a note of pride in the fact that he knew so many places. He said that on the train from New Haven he

* (1874-1925) American poet and critic.

[72]

noticed a young, good-looking couple with a baby. The woman was languid and weary. When he asked them where they came from, she said, "Portsmouth, New Hampshire, but I don't like the country around there." Mr. Frost told her something about the places and people around that section, but she showed little interest. Finally he asked where her home town was. "Texas," she said. "But you wouldn't know." Mr. Frost made her open her eyes by telling her a great deal about Texas, her country, and even mentioned some people she knew about. "I almost bought a house down there," he told her. She was regarding him with greater interest. Learning that her husband was a navy man and that they were due to move, he asked them where and learned that their destination was Key West. "I know Key West very well," he told them. "I almost bought a house down there." He went on to describe the place to them. "Not much doing, full of soldiers." He took a quiet enjoyment in their surprise and the fact that he could talk just as well about other parts of the country.

Everywhere he went the feeling was most friendly. Occasionally he would detect a note of distrust, and that he feared much. Once he noticed it when he went into a drugstore and heard a couple of boys whispering, "That's him!" There had been a robbery committed in the neighborhood recently, and Mr. Frost, a stranger, was one of the suspects. "Though a much-embarrassed druggist tried to make it easy for me: he talked to me a great deal and mentioned my name loudly for others to hear." Once in England, at a gathering of people, he had felt the flavor of disfavor. James Stephens was there, and he was one of Mr. Frost's friends. One man made the comment, "I hear, Mr. Frost, that in America it isn't green after July 1st." Stephens answered, "He comes from Vermont which means green all the year round." But the note of distrust was still there. On another occasion, he had been insulted by a man from Tennessee at some gathering in the South. Mr. Frost had made some light remark about the World War which was then going on, and the man replied, "I suppose you damned Yankees treat just as lightly the war you had with the South." Mr. Frost did not answer. But a man answered for him. (Mr. Frost did not remind him that his full name was Robert Lee Frost and that his family always had the strongest sympathy for the South.)

He mentioned a poem he had seen (in manuscript) by Robert Burns, a love poem written at the age of fifteen. On the manuscript, Burns had written, "I am not going to do this type any more until I have had some experience with girls."

Recently he had bought *Finnegan's Wake*, James Joyce's latest book, paying five dollars for it. Looking it over, he decided he was "out" five dollars. He did not understand it. In fact, the only thing he did understand was a quotation which he had previously learned and given to audiences as an example of obscurity. He had given it so many times that he was beginning to get a glimmer of what the man meant in it. Now he found it the only understandable part of the book.

He had been "dragged" to Bread Loaf. He had recently bought a farm near it, and some of the people from Bread Loaf were coming to this farm to play baseball. Years ago when the thing started he had been approached, but he had tried to steer clear of it. Yet they would not take "no" for an answer. They had taken him up there. He tried to get out of it once by saying he would not go unless they got Louis Untermeyer to take the poetry part of it. Louis accepted. Untermeyer was one of these men who could read an obscure poem one day and a week afterwards mention a certain line or a certain word in it. He had a great deal more patience with poems than Mr. Frost ever did.

Several times Mr. Frost mentioned the "spiritual realm of poetry." It was his contention that he had more to do with that than with the material end of it.

He jibed a little at Carl Sandburg and his "set formula." Sandburg first would give an audience a few definitions of poetry. Then he would recite a few poems. Then he would get out his guitar and sing a few ballads. He did all this over and over again.

He told us he had a friend in New Haven who was at work on a biography of a fellow named Josiah Willard Gibbs. Gibbs lived on a certain street. He never went anywhere all his life. He died at the same place. And yet he exerted a tremendous influence on a great many prominent people. Einstein said he was the greatest man in America. Through this account, Mr. Frost was making the point that one need not travel widely in order to be successful.

He talked for some time about his friend, Jack Wheelwright, "a strange but sincere poet." He was an architect. "I can almost see how he got himself killed by an automobile. He just rushed forward out of a house and into the street, impetuously." Mr. Frost remembered the time when there was a little party given for T. S. Eliot. Mr. Frost and Eliot both read their poems. Wheelwright was there. After a time he went out into another room and came back with some poems which he said he would like to read. This he did very strongly and apparently to the wonderment of the company. He had a queer face. There was nothing, however, of the phony about him. He had designed Robert Hillyer's house, a square, uninteresting place.

About *North of Boston*, he said, "It was T. E. Hulme who wanted me to change the title to *Yankee Eclogues*. Often, people in England would ask me what part of England I meant. They did not connect Boston with New England."

These and other topics he talked about. I listened until 11:30 and almost missed my train home. The whole evening had a dream-like quality about it, with that white-haired man backed by a fireplace, talking on and on about so many subjects, sliding into one after another with ease and enjoyment.

So many incidents: the pipes creaking with the steam in them, and Mr. Frost's humorous comment; the stuttering student who wanted to have a book autographed but was embarrassed to have to confess that he had picked it up in a secondhand store; the students addressing him as "Sir"; the muttering student behind me who continued to listen; the janitor prowling outside the door, wondering if we were ever going home.

So I left him, still talking, still glowing among his students before the unlighted fireplace while they hung upon every word he uttered.

CHAPTER VII

Mr. Frost at Home

I SAW HIM AGAIN on December 21, 1940. He came out on the porch and welcomed me in. For a long time I had been tingling in anticipation of this visit. Robert Frost would be alone, and I would be able to talk with him, undisturbed by any other person. I think I might be excused a little pride that I had been singled out for a special invitation to his Boston home. I had accepted with eagerness; and when the evening came, I arrived early, killing time by walking up and down Boston streets.

I had wondered about his Boston house. Earlier, hearing that I was to visit him, Mr. Holmes had told me that he spent the past summer in Mr. Frost's home at Shaftsbury, Vermont, and he gave me a description of the place. I copied it down, for I was very much interested in the type of home in which Mr. Frost lived:

"The house is a made-over farmhouse, white, with a brick-floored porch and a terrace with a low, wide rock wall, and it looks diagonally up the valley, with Shaftsbury itself the only sign of habitation anywhere. The grass and flowers are somewhat overgrown, or unplanted, because they had only just arrived. Inside the house, as we saw later, is the dining room, from which narrow stairs go up, and the kitchen door is on the left. Through a passage is the long living room, floor painted blue, and a large fireplace and oven, since this was once the kitchen and kitchen-bedroom. At the end opposite the door from the passage, bookshelves have been built-in either side of a window. There were two or three reddish Oriental rugs, and several Lankes woodcuts on the walls, a large water-color of fishing boats over the desk near the bookcase, and an oil of the Vermont hills at the opposite end of the room where another stairway goes up. There is a door going out onto the grass, almost opposite the fireplace, and a divan opposite the desk, and several chairs, wicker and otherwise. There are two large bedrooms on the first floor. In the dining room, the table of which was strewn with his papers and unanswered letters, there are several more Lankes woodcuts."

When Mr. Frost ushered me into his home in Boston, greeting me with his friendly smile, I remembered my friend's description. I looked carefully about me, making a mental comparison. Many easy chairs and a long divan were arranged about this room which apparently served as both a study and a library. I took off my coat and put it on the divan, but Mr. Frost urged me to put it in another place so that it would not seem as if I were getting ready to rush off again. Mr. Frost's desk was a beautiful piece: it looked like an antique of cherry or maple, very spacious. The remarkable thing about it was the seven drawers in the rear of the desk; there must have been seven in front, also. It was littered with papers and books and writing materials. There was a fine fireplace filled with unlighted birch logs. On the mantlepiece were several objects —a medal, a long dish containing a well-grown ivy, and a large vase of gladioli, zinnias, marigolds, and others. On a stand near the door was a large pot of wax begonias. Above the fireplace was a beautifully-drawn picture of chickadees on branches in the snow. This was the best picture in the place, though I noticed some woodcuts by Lankes, a steel engraving, and two old scenes of Inca civilization.

Mr. Frost had a dog with him, a sleek, affectionate English setter. On one side of the room, tall bookcases had been built into the wall, and they were almost entirely filled with books. Beside Mr. Frost's chair lay a bag full of notebooks and books. On little settees and on the desk were other books and magazines. A small radio stood on the floor.

Mr. Frost sat down in an old easy chair which was wrinkled and worn. As soon as I was comfortably seated, he commenced to sink down until his shoulders were almost as low as his knees. He did not move again except to get lower in his chair.

He started in by talking about poetry and what to look for in a poem. He said that the first thing he looked at was the rhyming—to see if it were strained, or if it flowed along without being artificial. The whole secret of the best rhyming is to make it so that the reader cannot tell which was thought of first. The mark of the poor writer was the obvious. He recalled a little poem of Ezra Pound's about skunk cabbage in which he used "crabbed age" as a rhyme for the name of this plant. There was no other reason for bringing it in except for rhyme, and this, in Mr. Frost's opinion, was a poor excuse.

"Now," said Mr. Frost, "let us take three quatrains and examine them carefully for the rhyming. There is Edwin Markham's

> He drew a circle that shut me out—
> Heretic, rebel, a thing to flout.
> But Love and I had the wit to win:
> We drew a circle that took him in!

"This poem is getting around a lot and has had much attention. But that will pass away in a few years. First line is good. Second, 'Heretic, rebel, a thing to flout.'—bad. You can see how he searched his brain for a proper rhyme, found 'flout' and stuck it in. Very weak. Third line is good again. Last line not very good. It is easy to see that he is bound up by the rhyming.

"Now take

> For He that worketh high and wise,
> Nor pauses in His plan,
> Will take the sun out of the skies
> Ere freedom out of man.

"Emerson. You can see how he got this poem. It is an epigram in two lines. He looked up at the sky, saw the sun and how much it was a part of the sky—then the thought of how much freedom was a part of him flashed into his mind. He compared the two. But he had to have two lines to rhyme with them. He picked out 'wise' and 'plan,' and they do not come anywhere near the top of the others. They are weak. They do not form a perfect working part of the rest of the lines. Remember that we go on line by line in poetry, building up from the idea, trying to make a rhyming that will not seem the tiniest bit strained.

"Now take Walter Savage Landor:

> I strove with none, for none was worth my strife;
> Nature, I lov'd, and next to Nature, Art;
> I warmed both hands before the fire of life;
> It sinks, and I am ready to depart.

"This is well-nigh perfect. Take the first line. He believed that. He was a rugged inidividual; he did struggle with people but he didn't know about it. (Threw a man out of his window and then looked out to see if his flowers had been hurt.) He might have taken a better way of saying the second line, but he didn't, and I admire him for that. It is all right. The rhyming is good."

I could see that he wanted to talk a great deal about poetry. I think I might have interrupted him in the act of writing, for there was a handwritten poem on the top of his pile of books.

When I spoke of the value of taking advantage of an environment, he said this:

"You know, we don't need to be original or inventive. You don't need to find new things. Just take the old things you find about you, the things people have known all their lives, and say them in your own style. That is the way. Call the attention to them. Be observant. In the work on the farm, notice the people, the way they cut up meat, harness horses, and the way they use words. Put them down. Don't worry about understanding people too much. If you work with them, observe, and talk with them, you will come to know enough for your poetry. Always use what you know about and don't write about foreign lands and foreign machines. Observe everything—that is the point I am stressing. For instance, I once came upon a rare orchis—the Calypso orchis. Perhaps you do not know it. I bent down and noticed how it was practically all seedpod—just a little tuft of flowers growing out of the end of the pod. Look at the fuzz on plants.

"There are two dangers that you are liable to run into. If you write too much, you are liable to drop into the rut of sameness—write poems that seem too near alike. If you don't write often enough, your wheels are apt to get rusty, and you may be unable to start again. There are some writers who wrote very little and very badly, and one wonders why they started at all. . . . Besides the rhyming and rhythm, you have to take care you don't pad your lines. Don't use unnecessary words. If you are writing a long poem, you must sustain yourself to the last ounce. Somewhere along the line, you are apt to fall down."

To my question about his early life, he started back at the beginning:

"I did a great deal of reading between the ages of fifteen and twenty-five. But I did not like college. I attended for a short time at Dartmouth and Harvard, but I didn't get my degree. My mother was teaching in a small country school, and from college I went home and helped her out. She took a class of smaller boys, and I took a class of larger boys. I taught off and on in little places—taught when I felt like it. I went about a great deal, went south, had something to do with a small newspaper for a while. Finally, I married, and my grandfather gave me a small farm in Derry, New Hampshire. He paid $1700 for it—$1727, to be exact, for the mortgage came to exactly $1700. There was some hay on the place, and we gave the owner an extra $25 for that, so that he would have some spending money. We had a tiny income from some money left to us—and with that and the farm, we stayed there for ten years.

"I had three hundred white Wyandottes; I knew something about the care of them, and I built a good henhouse for them. I learned to kill them for market, sticking them with a knife. In the summer, I hired out to a man, going around with him to various places and doing haying and plowing and tasks needing to be done. We were very poor, but we managed to get along. Moreover, we had a tenant who lived in half our house. He made a bargain with my grandfather over my head and seemed to think he was entitled to half of everything on the place—chickens, crops, the cow. It was he who milked the cow, and when he came to leave he handed her over to me, thinking that I was stuck since I had no knowledge of milking. But I learned milking on the spot.

"I stayed there for ten years. The taxes amounted to $30 a year—$300. I sold the farm for $1900. So it really cost me $100 for ten years' rent. Finally I started a little teaching again. It was at Pinkerton Academy in Derry. It had been noised around that my poems had been published a little, so the heads of the academy offered me a job. When it was learned that I had no degree, the teachers were inclined to look down on me. Moreover, I was heaped with work. I did thirty-five hours of classes a week, more than any other teacher in the school. The average was twenty-five hours a week. But I did fairly well for a while. Then I almost got a job as the head of a school. It was fortunate that I didn't, or else I might have been stuck there yet. It paid $3000 a year. It was I who persuaded them not to take me. 'I haven't a degree,' I said, 'and it wouldn't look well in the school advertising bulletins.' About this time, I sold my farm and was preparing to move from the country. But they persuaded me to teach one more year at a nearby school. I then packed up everything and went to England.

"I went to England with the material for several books. In every book I ever published, there is material from that early period. If I ever publish another book, there will be pieces in it from those first efforts.

"None of my children knew that I wrote poetry in those early years. It was not until I was thirty-eight that my oldest daughter knew about my writing.

"When I returned from England, I had published two books that had made a great deal of comment. But mine was a new thing. It was not always favorable comment. The conservative ones were handling me with kid gloves. For instance, the *Century*, which had never accepted any of my poems, treated my book gingerly. They found only one good poem in it, 'After Apple-Picking,' and they called attention to my rhyming 'comb' with 'home.' Ezra Pound shoved me into *Poetry*—reviews of my books; I don't think Harriet Monroe was very kindly, but he bullied her. In his reviews in her magazine, he quoted the very poems that she had rejected.

"I went to teaching again after a while. First, I went to Michigan, and did nothing for a couple of years. Then I went to Amherst, had brief and far-between classes for a time, and did nothing for eight years. Now I am at Harvard. But my classes are very informal, as you know, and only once a week.

I don't like the idea of teaching poetry. Most of my students are not poets at all."

He talked a little about college-teacher poets, his estimate of their work. Once he suddenly opened up with a barrage of questions, returning to my work, the people I knew who were interested in poetry. All the while he was asking these questions, Mr. Frost's face was lighted up and animated. He seemed a part of the chair in which he was sitting, but his quiet eyes peered out at me steadily from under his heavy eyebrows. He would study me for long periods of time; then his eyes would wander back over the room and the ceiling. Now and then he would ruffle up his white hair with his hands, and I understood how it got that tousled, uncombed appearance. He talked almost without pause, the changes on his face growing more frequent.

He asked me if I would like to go to college again. Would I be able to settle down beneath the dictum of those in power? That is what irked him most at a college. When he entered Harvard, he avoided the English courses as much as possible, concentrating on Latin and Greek. He didn't think I needed to go to college. "You could learn by yourself. But you would never be able to teach without a degree. Go your own way; that is the only thing. Don't let people push you around too much. Discipline yourself. Did you ever read Aristotle's *Poetics?* It would do you good to tackle some heavy reading now and then. Go deep into philosophy and think about it. Read things that are beyond you. In early life, I myself did a great deal of reading. Now I do little, relying on knowledge of new books from hearsay."

It was evident that Mr. Frost had forgotten some of the things he had said in previous talks; he repeated himself. He brought up the question of religion, asking me what my denomination was. He said it would not do any harm to go to church now and then, but not to make a habit of it. Out in the country, there would likely be a lot of "hellraisers"; it would be interesting to drop in on churches here and there, to listen to the wheels going around in the minds of the ministers. He told me about his own upbringing. He had been baptized a Presbyterian, although his father was an atheist, using the name of God only in profanity. His mother was a Universalist, as her folks had been before her. Later, he had been baptized into the Swedenborgian faith. His mother had worried about him. He had a great many friends who were ministers or were connected with church work. He did not think any less of them for that. He did not go in heavily for religion—but he did not consider the church a bad thing. His was a waiting and hoping attitude:

> There may be little or much beyond the grave
> But the strong are saying nothing until they see.

"If you are going deeply into poetry, give your whole self to it—go the whole hog. Too many take it carefully, and fail. If it is to be your life, make everything else subordinate to it. It was Bill Sloane's* constant cry: 'Too many *little* books of verse about, scattered around the literary landscape. The books were by people who did not put their whole lives, ideas, flesh and blood into them. They played safe. They were always minor poets.' I started in early with my poetry. I did not like to be told how to go about it because I thought I had the intelligence to understand. After all, *there* was the poem on the printed page. Certain things were going on there. You should be able to get it—the rhyming, the idea, the reason for the being of the poem. There might be a great deal. For instance, what did Emerson mean when he said, 'Evil will bless and ice will burn,' in 'Uriel'? But one should be able to learn what goes on.

"Sometimes I have a little spell of writing. I have always been much afraid that one poem led to another. I don't want a

* William M. Sloane, III, Frost's publisher from 1939 to 1946.

logical sequence between the poems. I don't want the power of facility that would make me write a poem too easily.

"Better do nothing except when you get an urge. But you can wait for the urge to work so assiduously that you never start again. You have got to rush it a little.

"When a poet is in the mood and he gets stopped, he gets suicidal; but then, you get to know that something will start you again. You begin to hear little voices like hallucinations, many going on around you. You begin to phrase your feelings. All this you know. Words haunt you. It starts again, or else it doesn't. Most people complain that they never find time—and then they are in a fine fix."

He had many other things to say that evening. One topic was the teaching of poetry. Hillyer had been trying that—the teaching of versification. The idea was that if you followed all the rules of the game, you would become a poet. But it seems that you always become a minor one. No really great poet came out of a class in versification. As John Gould Fletcher said, "Why should I teach anyone? I learned from no one." But Hillyer continued with his courses, and people came out of them with a knowledge of the rules of poetics.

He thumbed through his books musingly. He did not regard them as too much a part of him. "I suppose they are, though," he said. His early poems stood off from him a bit because he had forgotten so much about them through the years.

When I brought out my copy of the *Complete Poems* and requested an autograph, he said, "Gladly. Would you like me to copy something from the poems?" I said it would make me very happy if he would copy the first poem in his book—an eight-line poem. He commenced writing the poem from memory.

I watched this man, Robert Frost, intent over his book. His face changed strangely. He no longer seemed the old man who had been previously talking to me about poetry and poets.

"Well, I hope to see you again. I am not a steady letter-writer; you won't get many letters. But I hope you will send me some more poems occasionally."

Going down the steps . . . "Good-bye and good luck. Keep up with your poetry. Put yourself into it—that is the best thing to do, the best way of getting along. You are a good poet. You are one of the few I ever told that to."

I went out of the building, hearing the door shut behind me.

CHAPTER VIII

The Visit During the War

O N JANUARY 14, 1942, I was in Boston, Massachusetts, and had been invited to the home of Robert Frost
on Brewster Street in Cambridge. At the time, I was in the
United States Army, working at the recruiting office on
Columbia Terrace in Back Bay.

After a subway ride, I arrived in Cambridge and was at his
home a little after six in the evening. Two of his students were
just on the point of leaving, and from their talk I gathered
that one was a divinity student and the other a doctoral candi-
date. I was bothered a little bit when I realized they were
laughing heartily at almost every word Mr. Frost uttered,
even at the parts that were not particularly funny. I had the
feeling that they were trying mightily to make him enjoy
their conversation and prolong it.

When we were alone, he continued in this very talkative
and cheerful mood. The session with his students apparently
had put him into a very friendly and jovial frame of mind,
which continued throughout the duration of our talk.

After a few minutes, he jumped up and said, "How about
some supper?" Without waiting for me to answer, he proceeded to go out and prepare it. It was a temptation to have
followed him to the kitchen and to have watched the poet
acting the role of cook, but I did not think it would be pru-
dent.

While he was rattling the pans in the kitchen, I spent the time looking over a large collection of anthologies on a library shelf. There were many which were new to me. As I thumbed through them, I noted that each had the work of Mr. Frost included.

He called me into a little alcove to supper, and I was surprised at what he had prepared. There were two lamb chops on my plate and a mixture of rice and something else, a little chicken, I think. There was smoked cheese as a side dish. (He commented that this hickory smoked cheese was a favorite of his.) Fruit, pickles, crackers, and candy were the other delicacies on the table of this famous poet. When he finished the meal, he left the dishes on the table; he seemed anxious to get back to the parlor and talk.

As soon as we were seated, he said, "What is the latest about your manuscript?" I had mentioned in a letter that I had been trying to sell something to a publisher.

"I have a final word, Mr. Frost," I said. "It isn't very encouraging."

I handed him the long letter of rejection and watched him read it slowly. He followed the words with some grumbling and snorts of disgust.

"Why, this is nonsense!" he burst out. "For one thing he is trying to make the rejection easy by all these words. Why doesn't he come out and say that you did not get enough votes from the staff. When he says here that the book is 'too good to be published,' he means that it would not be appealing to large numbers of people. It won't sell. But he doesn't tell you that."

After grumbling some more about this letter and rereading it, he said, "I'm seeing my publisher next week; I'll talk to him about your work. I would like to have a copy of this, too."

He asked me if I had any poems with me, and when I pulled out a batch, he asked me to read some of them. First I read what I considered the best, and then he said, "Let me try one!" and he took a turn.

In the course of our discussion of the poems, a remarkable thing happened—or what seemed a stroke of good luck to me. He picked out two of the poems and proceeded to revise them. The first one (about a country kitchen) he felt was not complete. It had some excellent and sharp detail which was the framework of poetry, but it was not strong enough philosophically. Somehow, the personal element must be introduced, and he told me how he would accomplish this. He said, "I would put myself in command of the dawn and all the people sleeping in the house. I would use the expression, 'thrusting the dawn upon them.' In that way you have the possibilities of a powerful poem."

He continued, "Now in this 'Last Haying' poem, you have hit upon a great idea, but you haven't carried it far enough. You have a striking opportunity to say something moving and original in presenting the picture of the clouds being put away. I would use 'barn of darkness' as a line. I would stress the 'wheels under the wagon rumbling.' But I like the way you handle the idea in some of the lines; several of the lines falter, but many of them go on their way inevitably. You are catching the trick of drawing parallels, and that is one of the great secrets, the great secrets."

He paused for a moment and then looked down again at the poem. Finally, he said, "This is the way I think it should go." He proceeded to give me a new version of the poem, using some of the expressions he had already suggested and making up others as he went along, but keeping to the original rhythm of the poem.

I was astonished and delighted. It was a great temptation to pull out my notebook and put down these words, but I did not do so.

He put aside the poems and began a long talk on the "how" of writing poetry, and this was the best part of the evening.

There were three items in a poem: the idea or the point, the details, the technique. Once he gets the idea, the poet should think about it and draw a parallel. The classic example is Whitman's poem written while he was observing a spider. The spider kept throwing out a filament, kept throwing it out until finally after a long while it caught on something. Then the spider hastened away on his business. The mind of man has done the same thing. It keeps throwing out lines, keeps throwing out ideas through the reaches of space until it finally hits upon death, and having found that, it hurries away into the darkness to be gone forever.

Mr. Frost continued by stressing that these ideas should be followed. You, as a poet, are able to catch them with the edges of the mind, and with one you make a point in a poem, a reason for writing. The details fill in the sides of the poems —and this is why an extremely observant eye is worthwhile. "You should teach yourself to think more and catch upon ideas more. But you are doing well right now, and the good poems show you are on the right way."

He added, "One does not need to write long poems. A poet might be suited to short poems just as other poets might be suited to long ones. Proof of that might be in the work of Dickinson and Whitman. Some people have executive minds, and they have to do lengthy writing and tell lengthy stories when they talk. Others are very short in speech and can say just as much in a few words."

He mentioned his friend Will Christman and how he got started late in life to write poetry. "That is remarkable and ties in with what we have been saying. When he had time in his old age to think and gather ideas, he wrote some impressive work. He was free to write, and we are not always free."

He had much to say when I mentioned poetry societies. He said, "People think they come to them for help. I do not encourage that idea. I pity the writers who attend them; I pity them more than I pity the boys in the army. They lead such futile lives as they listen to discussion and argue about poetry. They are not able to do any worthwhile work themselves. It does not do a poet much good to be able to get up and offer facile words of criticism about poetry. So many of these people are so educated that they cannot write. They are tied down by their wealth of knowledge.

"But let us look at the poetry societies this way. When I come to read my poems to a group, do I ask the people for criticism? It would spoil the poems if I did. It happened to me once in England when I had been invited to read. Someone got up and offered some criticism on my reading. I was so shocked I did not know how to insult him."

In regard to lecturing, he felt very often that he was giving a poor lecture; and at other times he had the feeling he was giving his best words. Some lectures he thought would be better off if no one ever recorded them.

I commented that some day I hoped to write about him and his talks. His reply was, "Good, but I hope you pick the best ones."

The evening went on very pleasantly, and I had a feeling of regret when it was time for me to go. I would have liked to have stayed and helped him with the dishes, but I knew he would not stand for it. He shook hands warmly and urged me to drop in on him again. But I was to be transferred in a few days, and I did not see him again until he came to Washington to visit with his daughter Lesley.

CHAPTER IX

Round Table in Washington

O N A DAY in November, 1943, I attended a reception given Mr. Frost in Washington, D.C. Service in the army had kept me from seeing him for many months, but I was now preparing to go overseas, and the sight of the poet in the home of his daughter was a pleasant memory to take with me. I was given the opportunity, also, of seeing him again in the company of many people and of watching his reactions to them.

There were thirty or so talkative and restless men and women. (Earlier, Miss Frost had confided that most of the people would leave in a short while and that I and a small group would have a good opportunity to talk with him.) I remember feeling lost and cast adrift upon all this babble of tongues. I was introduced to the wife of the Attorney General, to a Justice of the Supreme Court, to officials from the Smithsonian Institute, to a General from Hawaii, to a teacher of fiction writing, and to an editor of the *Washington Post*. But I took little part in the exchange of talk. I was more interested in watching Robert Frost, who stood by the fireplace and was swamped with handshakers.

His daughter Lesley was nervously welcoming each guest. So many people seemed absorbed in her father that I preferred to keep in the background as much as possible. When I finally did shake hands with him, he turned to his right-hand neighbor and said, "Here is one of the boys I brought up. He goes to New York and wins all the prizes." He went on to speak very pleasantly of books and poetry acceptances.

Since the time I had first gotten to know him in John Holmes' sitting room, he had lost none of his jovialness. Having just arrived from Florida, he looked very brown and rested. His appearance did not show that he had just recovered from an attack of pneumonia. He had been working on some verse plays—*A Masque of Reason* and *A Masque of Mercy*. Even though he was close to seventy now, the creative spirit had not dimmed.

After most of the people had gone, Lesley organized a sort of round table with Mr. Frost at the head of it. We were only too glad to sit and listen.

In the middle of the table was a vase of jonquils, tulips were on the mantlepiece, and in back of Mr. Frost, a large picture looked down on him. As usual, he slid down in his chair until his head almost rested on the back of it. His feet were doubled underneath, upon the rung, and he looked very sleepy as he talked. In fact, his eyes closed at times, as, in his hesitant fashion, he told stories and kept us interested for hours. In front of him was a package of Phillip Morris cigarettes, and, as he talked, he unwrapped the cellophane from it and twisted it in his hands. For hours he twisted that cellophane, and when the evening was over, there was a little pile of bits of cellophane on the table.

He started out by telling a favorite story, about how he met Mrs. Biddle, wife of a Washington official, on the train, and had a talk of a few minutes with her. When she left, the Negro porter came up and said, "Well, I see that you poets get together." "Oh, you knew that we are poets?" said Frost. "Yes. I've read your poems. Some of us read them. And I want you to know that we are behind you!" Telling this anecdote, Mr. Frost chuckled and said this was comforting, perhaps an example of democracy.

One of the men present was an official from the War Production Board, having a great deal to do with the doling out of paper for publishing concerns. He launched a discussion about books, the fifty million *more* books printed this year than last with *less* paper available! The increase was in the pocket books especially. And Cardinal O'Connell of Boston had presented quite a problem with his four-volume work on something or other. Mr. Frost disagreed with him on one point, on the value of widespread, cheap publishing. He said that he himself differed from many of the poets like Sandburg, Lindsay, and Robinson in that he had had always a well-made-up book put out. The publisher, the designer, the artist —all were good. And the artist especially would not understand what he was talking about when he spoke of "hastily-printed books." Libraries were important. People were not so cramped as others would have them believe. I think it nettled Mr. Frost a little bit when the other drew a picture of a postwar world where homes would be stored on the backs of cars, and libraries would consist of tiny editions or possibly pages flashed upon a screen.

He talked a bit on the definitions of words—how people were loosely scattering words around like "democracy" and even "love" without knowing exactly what was meant. As an example, he took the word "love" and showed how it was pushed around in various languages—how loosely its meaning was held. He first met loose usage of the word in New England when his aunt, complaining about his lack of appetite, said, "Don't you love your food?" She meant "like," naturally. He said that through his life he had come to the conclusion that it was not wise to be for or against anything. Too many people were that way. Right now, there was much talk about the nations, or certain nations, loving each other. Of course, this is not true. A Britisher is a Britisher, and an American is an American.

In his early youth in San Francisco, he had been a "free

trade democrat," simply because his father had been one before him. His father was "an editorial democrat" and sneered at any idea of a tariff. He had been a Democrat all his life.

Mr. Frost had read but one book in two or three years—Jessie Stuart's* latest novel about Private Tussie. He had liked it and had been impressed because Stuart had gone ahead and told a story, instead of being like Caldwell and Steinbeck who were reformers and could not write without trying to reform.

He had much to say about notable idealists—the painter Ed Bruce for one, who wanted everybody to paint, and whenever someone came to his door and said he could paint, Bruce would support him while he painted. He helped hundreds of people. But then when he died all his work died with him; the exhibitions were closed, and the paintings were burned. He spoke of Judge James M. Landis** who suffered for the sorrows of the world. And he told of a friend who thought the Indians should be given back the lands they had been robbed of. This friend had done much for the American Indian. "The reservations are expanding," he announced triumphantly to Mr. Frost. "You mean they might reach out?" asked Mr. Frost with a frightened look. The other nodded. "Yes. The Indian is going ahead." "Of course, this is all nonsense," concluded Mr. Frost. "No matter what happens we are not going back to Europe. We may raise the Indian up to where he begins to assert himself, and then we run him back into the ditch again."

I noted Lesley Frost's delighting over all of us, watching our expressions. Now and then she would ask her father to tell something she wanted us to hear. She told only one story herself—about the artist friend of hers who had painted Joe Louis. Joe came to her house with two of his bodyguards—enormous men. They read magazines while she painted Joe. When she asked him to show his muscles, he said, "If my mus-

* (1907-   ) Author of *Man with the Bull-Tongued Plow*.
** (1899-1964) Former Dean of Harvard Law School and friend of FDR.

[*96*]

cles showed, I would be musclebound." "And brains?" she asked. He looked at her and said, "There are no brains connected with boxing. It is all training." Mr. Frost elaborated a bit on this story, agreeing with Joe that muscles did the thinking and not the brains.

He told a story "off the record." This concerned the time he met Henry Wallace and chided him by saying, "Well, at least, Mr. Wallace, I can give a lecture without dragging God into it!" Later, Wallace was telling Lesley how he had written a lecture to be delivered in New York before some bishops of the Episcopal Church. He had taken the lecture to FDR for comment. The President had handed it back saying that it sounded all right. "Are you sure that I haven't mentioned God too many times?"asked Wallace. "You know, Robert Frost tells me I can't write without mentioning God." FDR threw back his head and laughed. He said, "Henry, once I tried leaving God out of one of my speeches. And there was so much repercussion that I have never dared to try it again!"

Mr. Frost seemed to be enjoying himself hugely. He laughed like a child and even did a little play-acting as he imitated his talk with someone. In one case it was with the ten-year-old daughter of Judge Landis. She must have been a precocious child, for she (like her father) lost sleep over the sorrows of the world. She once came to the poet and said, "Mr. Frost, what do you think of Archibald MacLeish's *America Was Promises?*" He imitated her manner of speaking when he replied, "Don't you think there is a little too much accent on the 'was'?" She replied, "Yes. You may be right."

As the talk progressed, Mr. Frost became warmed up. The minutes went by swiftly. No one made any mention of time except Lesley, who once reminded her father that no one had had lunch. But he went on with the talk, and no one thought of leaving. Apparently they were not hungry for food; they were eager to listen to one of the most interesting persons in the world. Perhaps some laughed too heartily. However, I do think they were sincerely drawn to this man and his talk.

He spoke of his neighbors in Vermont, the Billings, the Crams, the Grayce family, the Dragons. The Dragons particularly were a vital lot. Part Indian, their name a contraction of "dragoon," the family was scattered over several states. One of them worked on Mr. Frost's place but never did a great deal. Mr. Frost could not get rid of him. But he did like to tell his visiting friends that he had two horses and a Dragon on the farm.

The Billings were Protestants, the Dragons were Catholics. And the Crams were atheists. The Billings were always doing their best for their little church. One day, one of them came to Mr. Frost and said, "That anvil you have hanging around would do much for the war effort. May we have it?" Mr. Frost said "no." Then he wormed out the information that she did not want the anvil for the war effort at all but for raising money to support the church. She was doing good in a sneaky way. The Crams, on the other hand, were godless. One of them earlier had gone to church off and on. Finally, the minister had spoken to him: "I see that you come to church now and then. Perhaps you would like to contribute something to its support." Cram snorted, "God damn it! Why don't you charge admission!" And he never went to a church again.

He made a strong impression on me when he said, "This difficult place in which we find ourselves. This trial ground." Whether or not he meant it in the religious sense I do not know. I do not think so. He once referred to the present company as "probably godless." He spoke of the Quakers as a group of people who would not fight because they were all preachers. He mentioned Brigham Young's monument in a little ghost town in southern Vermont. A sarcastic inscription was put there by one of his enemies, he believed.

[*98*]

He spoke of God in another story. A friend had married a Southern wife, even though his father had commanded a Negro regiment during the Civil War. "Now," said Mr. Frost, addressing both husband and wife, "I would like to know this: in all your discussions, what did you finally decide? Whose side was God on in the Civil War?" The wife spoke up and said, "My father was a bishop, and he always said that God was on the side of the South." "That's all I wanted to hear," said Mr. Frost.

Sisters can be stubborn. He recalled that when he was seventeen, he was required to do some Latin homework. His sister was with him in a room on the third floor. They found they interfered with each other's studying. He finally picked up his sister, put her outside, and locked the door, although she had claimed half the room was hers. She immediately climbed out on the tile roof surrounding the building and walked around until she came to the window of the room. She was in danger, so Mr. Frost pulled her into the room. "Just to show you how stubborn sisters can be," said Mr. Frost. "Three stories, straight down!" One lady exclaimed on this, saying that she felt sure the sister must have made a great success in life: she must be successful even now! "She may be," said Mr. Frost. "She is dead now."

When asked about possible publication of his verse play about Job, he said he did not think it would be published until he had completed the other one. He talked for a few minutes on this play, saying that some people would consider it blasphemous.

He mused over the fact that there was a time when the common man was a laughing matter. The clown of the court was a common man of the streets. They would bring him in to laugh at him. But now the situation is reversed. The kings get the laugh (like the Prince of Wales falling off his horse). The common man has grown in importance. Mr. Frost went on to say that for a while it was believed that kings and noblemen were the only ones who had sorrows. The common man always slept well nights. The rich sometimes had their dainty sorrows. But came a time when the poor demanded a share of these "dainty sorrows." He seemed to like to dwell on this theme of the "common man," a term which had recently come into great popularity. He had noted that the problems of the common man were discussed most often in the circles of the rich and famous, where they actually were out of touch with him as much as possible.

There was a man who came to a little town in Vermont and was hired to teach. But he soon got into trouble by telling his twelve-year-old students that they were underprivileged. ("As if all students at that age are not underprivileged! They can't marry; they can't vote; they can't do a lot of things.") He was fired. But he complained to Dorothy Canfield Fisher and Sarah Cleghorn about it, contending that the children were not in good homes. Instead of investigating the matter themselves, they sent their minister. When he popped in on the Billings' family and said, "I hear that you are not giving your children the proper upbringing," the mother's retort was, "And I ask what's to prevent it?"

In his whimsical fashion, Mr. Frost reeled off story after story, sometimes with a great deal of fire and spirit, as, for instance, in this one: "There is nothing so disconcerting or irritating as when milking a cow the animal kicks over the milkpail or puts her foot into it. One day, one of these Polish farmers was milking when the cow slapped him with her tail and kicked over the pail. He was so angry that he looked around for a pitchfork with which to kill the cow, and finding none handy, he leaped upon the cow's back and, putting his teeth in her back, he bit clear through to the backbone. When her bellow of anguish was heard all over the neighborhood, he shouted, 'Well, damn you! Who begun it?' Mr.

Frost told this story with an activity and a shout that startled us.

A lawyer friend of his had once told him that we know everything there is to know about food. "Everything?" asked Mr. Frost. "Well, almost everything," the other confessed. "Probably ten percent is unknown. It is the same way with poverty. We are going to do away with poverty—or almost all. It may be ten percent or so that won't be reached." "But," said Mr. Frost, "you must remember that poetry is *with* that ten percent!" The man jumped at that. "You mean," he said loudly, "that poetry has a vested interest in poverty?" "In the words of your parliamentary law," answered Mr. Frost, "the answer is in the affirmative. Poverty and sorrow."

He recalled that he had had one colored student in his class at Michigan. There were a dozen students in the class, each taking a turn in leading the class discussion. When it came the Negro's turn, he was one of the best. At times in recent years, Mr. Frost had received pamphlets of some sort that this man had written. He was now high up in the medical profession.

He told a story about the man who lived in a shack simply because he was there permitted to spit on the stove when he wanted to.

So the talk went on for hours—books and people, farming, religion, colored people, politics, Vermont, neighbors, poetry, sorrows, Hervey Allen. He liked to talk about the latter, how tempestuous he was, "always fighting the government." Once on the train, he had demanded a pillow; when he was refused, he telephoned ahead for one. Two officials boarded the train later with a pillow for him. Hervey was like that, always kicking up a rumpus. People thought of him as a novelist. Yet he had written many books of poetry.

Robert Frost made us forget time. The figure in the chair slipped down further, and the little pile of twisted cellophane grew. When we took our leave, he said, "Let us hope that the war will soon be over."

CHAPTER X

Mr. Frost in Cambridge

I DID NOT SEE Robert Frost again until after the war. As an infantryman in General Patton's Third Army, I went to France and Germany. His daughter Lesley went to Madrid, Spain. Mr. Frost himself went from Harvard to a new job at Dartmouth in New Hampshire. He did his usual rounds of lecturing, spent time in his Florida home, and finished his verse plays as well as more poetry for a new book.

Back home in November of 1945, I received my discharge from the army. On December 3, I went to Boston, and taking a chance I called the private telephone number Mr. Frost had given me. To my surprise, he answered and promptly invited me to come over that evening.

When I appeared at the door, he welcomed me in his usual hearty fashion. Although he had aged considerably, much of his great activity and interest was still there. His smile of pleasure was very warming; I had not known its like for a long time. Boyishly he ushered me into his study and began to fire questions to me at a rapid rate.

He was much interested in my campaign ribbons (I still had on my uniform). I found myself hard pressed to keep up with his questions about my impressions of foreign lands, of work and war, of experiences in Germany, and of the reactions of our own men. I held nothing back. He claimed that all my experiences were valuable material for future writing; the clothing of unimportant events would gradually drop from the most vivid days so that I would remember in time only the sparkling, worthwhile incidents. Such stuff inspired poetry. His own poetry-writing at present was nothing more than memories that had been cleaned and whittled to sharpness by the passage of time.

I owned something to be proud of, he thought. It would be more important later. To stress this point still more, he spoke of the blizzard of 1888, one of the greatest storms the country ever had. Mr. Frost had newly arrived from California, so he was not prepared for the mass of snow-piles everywhere. He now remembered more and more vividly the feeling of intense cold in the air, the sight of the snowfields, the drifts of whiteness higher than his head which he had to shout over to someone on the other side, and all the stark beauty of the countryside that he saw on a morning between Lawrence and Haverhill.

It was hard to keep him away from the subject of the war, and though we would talk about other topics for a while, he would return to this general subject. I had to satisfy his intense curiosity with answers to questions like these: "What was it like for a man to be hit by a bullet? . . . What were your thoughts and feelings on a battlefield? . . . How did the German women treat you? . . . Did you meet any other writers or newspapermen in Europe? . . . What was your reaction when the war ended? . . . What was your impression of the countryside of Germany? . . . Did you have any narrow escapes? . . . What did you and the other boys talk about? . . . How did the officers treat you? . . . Did you hate your officers and the enemy? . . . "

These sample questions made me think later that I could have found no better example of a poet's curiosity. He had started out by saying, "I have heard a great deal about the war. Now I want to hear it from you, and I think you'll tell me the truth."

Eventually he stopped his questions, and I asked him about his early writing.

He said that he wrote his first poem at the age of fifteen. He was on his way home from school when he started to write this long ballad. The next day, he laid the poem on the desk of the literary editor of the school magazine. It was published shortly thereafter. He wrote off and on for many years, seeming to produce the same quantity year after year. He told the story of how he had developed Harriet Monroe into a "friendly enemy." Just before leaving for England, he had sent her a group of poems, and he soon received them back. They found their way across the water to him. When Ezra Pound came to review his book in *Poetry*, he quoted from several of the rejected poems as prime examples of Mr. Frost's work. Later, talking before a club he told this story—how it was impossible for him to get into *Poetry* except through a review. Miss Monroe finally heard of it.

He went to England with his family about 1912 and stayed there three years. This family of four resolved to find a thatched cottage somewhere in which they might live cheaply and earn their way through writing. The cost of the three years for the four of them was $3600. When they landed back in New York, they had fifty cents between them. But his book had been published in America and was finding its way around. He was asked to give several readings, one of them in Portland, Maine. This led to a curious coincidence.

He had a friend named Charles Cardin, a high school classmate. He was more resolute than Mr. Frost in his senior year. Mr. Frost did not know where he was going or what he wanted to do, but this fellow said he was going to medical college, get a good practice, earn enough money to be independent, and then write poetry, something that would make a name for himself like *Paradise Lost*. "All right," said Mr. Frost. "I'll meet you here when you and I are forty, and we'll see how far we have gotten."

Years later on the train to Portland, a man across the aisle said to Mr. Frost, "I know a man who knows the man who wrote that book you are carrying." "Well, I wrote the book," said Mr. Frost. "The man is Dr. Cardin," said the newcomer. Instantly, Mr. Frost remembered their bargain of twenty years before. "Oh yes, I have a date with him in Lawrence this year. How is he?" He learned subsequently that the man had a small practice in Haverhill and that he was not doing very well. Drink had about gotten him. "So," concluded Mr. Frost, "you can't plan for writing like that. If you figure on getting leisure time later for creative work, that time may never come."

I asked him if he had any qualms about speaking. Speaking was nothing to worry about, he thought. The audience is watching for you to live up to certain things. He did not make his first talk until he was thirty-eight. In school and out, he had dodged and ducked every opportunity to speak, even when he was doing his first part-time teaching assignment at Pinkerton Academy. Finally, he was cornered. His first chore consisted of a responsive reading in chapel.

"Have you read much poetry?" he asked me suddenly. "When you read a poem, do you ask yourself, 'Does this poem do all for me that it is supposed to do?' In writing a poem, it is nothing more than a lucky stroke—or a good pitch as in baseball. The art of throwing a curve ball. Looking back at a poem, you sometimes think, 'I might have made a better job than that, made a better throw.' When you curve the poem into being, you hope fervently that it breaks right."

He thought the thing for the poet of the world of today was to go his way alone and carve out his path. Everything would beset him, even his best friends, trying to make him write to please them. If a poet could be independent and stubborn, not swayed by prejudices and the tantrums of the day, the scorns and unmeaning words of societies and people, if he would stand on his own feet and plug away, not copying others, he might accomplish his work and make his mark. But it was all difficult and dark. A strange, terrible life.

It struck me that all his life he had tried to live up to what he had just said.

After a minute of silence, he seized the dictionary, saying that he had intended all day to look up the word "fraternize." As he thumbed the pages, I studied him carefully. He had taken his usual position in an armchair, slumping as far down as possible, his head pressed up against the chair-back. His face was square and fleshy, with heavy-lidded eyes. The skin of his face had lost much of its brownness; his nose was rather wide-nostrilled and flat. His hair was a scraggly white mass all over his head. His clothes at the time were very dusty, as if he had been searching around in an attic. His arm had crept around the back of his chair. That stubborn lower lip explained a lot.

I remembered what he had once said about "getting rid of convictions." Earlier in life when he was eighteen or nineteen, he had had a lot of "convictions" and had become tangled up with them. For instance, he had taken a serious interest in phrenology. When a phrenologist examined him and couldn't find a certain bump in the middle of the top of his head it worried him quite a bit. Now he had lost his "convictions," he said. However, I had not taken this statement very seriously. In past conversations with him, I had found him a stonewall of convictions, adhering to them firmly. I remembered something else he had said: "You can't push me very well. I don't roll easily."

As the evening grew late, he let his thoughts wander from subject to subject, and I listened attentively to the words that flowed from him.

He said that in high school he had played football. He had played for Lawrence against Haverhill. But he was too light (140 pounds), and it had not been good for him. He suffered for some time with stomach trouble because of his football playing, but he had never given up athletics. On his farm in Vermont he had a softball game going with members of the Middlebury conference. He had played tennis frequently with Louis Untermeyer. Last year, in spite of "rough spots," he had played softball and tennis and had suffered no ill effects.

Speaking of Mr. Untermeyer reminded him that he had once visited the critic at his home in the Catskills; he was in the act of going through a sheaf of three hundred poems, looking for poetry for the *American Mercury*. He handed over a pile of them to Mr. Frost and offered ten cents apiece for all the good poems he might discover. Mr. Frost, however, found him very reluctant to accept any of his choices. Finally, he did take two. But he remained firm against Robert P. Tristram Coffin, whom Mr. Frost thought ought to be accepted. More than half of the three hundred poems sounded as if they were written by the same school of poetry.

He spoke of Daniel Webster. He talked of him as the "great conciliator." Webster did not want a war between the North and the South, and like Chamberlain, he would go to any measure to prevent it. "I wonder if history will put him in the same class with Chamberlain? Lincoln, on the other hand, went just one step further. When he sent troops to Fort Sumter in South Carolina, he was being a radical. Of course, the land belonged to South Carolina, and we had no right to send troops there. The Southern states were nothing more than small nations and had a right to secede from a Union in which they did not believe. But it was something we could not afford to allow them to do. It would be unthinkable to have two separate nations squabbling on each other's borders. So we had to disregard what was right and go to war."

He suggested that I come to Dartmouth. "Just browse around. Attend any class you like. Study what you least know. If I were going to college at your age, I would take up Latin, early English, French, biology, history. But no modern English. You might even come to Bread Loaf in the summertime. You won't have to show any of your work. Just listen to what is going on. Some people enjoy having their work torn to pieces, but I know you wouldn't be in that class."

Speaking again of Dartmouth, he said, "I don't really know what they have me there for. Three weeks in the winter; three weeks in the spring. I just talk with the boys." He mused, "But everybody watches you. If you are a minister, they watch to see if you live up to the traditions of the pulpit. If you are a baseball pitcher, you must live up to the rules. If you are a poet, they scan you constantly for flaws."

He asked me if I had seen any praying in the army when the going was difficult. I said that I had. He said he did not see that it did much good to pray at the front, especially if you had not prayed before. "God would be too busy to mess around with such. But prayer did not do any harm. It never paid to ridicule anyone who prayed. But what was the use of it?"

When I finally left, he asked me to come and see him again. He said I had given him a lot to think about. I left him with an elated feeling, resolving to visit him again at the first opportunity.

CHAPTER *XI*

A Visit and a Lecture

A MONTH OR SO later I saw him again. Both of us had been very busy during the winter; my main object was to get myself organized after the war. Since I was to be in the vicinity of Boston for a time, I determined to try to see him again. In January of 1946, I called him at his Cambridge home and made an appointment. I carried to Boston several books to be autographed.

He welcomed me heartily, as he had always done. The big house was apparently hard to heat, for there was little more than a study and a bedroom open to warmth. The place, however, was very cozy and quiet. Mr. Frost seemed a little thinner than when I last saw him. I was struck anew by the broadness of his upper lip and how high his nose was on his face. The nose was perhaps out of proportion in such a heavy man. His horn-rimmed glasses lent him a different look. They were new, and he had broken them on the first trial by rolling on them. But he could still keep them on after a fashion. He said it irked him to find that he could not distinguish an eight from a zero in a telephone book anymore. Glasses bothered him, but he supposed he had to make use of them.

I looked about his study. There was a big pile of Christmas cards in the corner. Unopened packages of books lay on the floor. On his desk was a box of candy. On all sides of me stood the same high bookcases, rows and rows of many titles.

I saw solid rows of philosophical works, shelves devoted to Latin volumes, thick and varied books of history, and, of course, works of poetry everywhere. It looked like an interesting library; he told me he had similar libraries in every place he owned. Beside his big easy chair lay his notebooks and papers. When I came in, I may have interrupted his work upon a long piece of poetry, for I noted handwritten pages on top of the pile. It looked like dialogue. I wondered at the wealth of material these notebooks and papers must have represented. In the corner was a telephone with the longest cord I had ever seen. I imagined Mr. Frost must have taken that telephone from room to room in order to have it close at hand.

Nearby was a small Webster's dictionary which he had been using. He sat there for a while, hunched in his chair, thumbing the pages at the back. Seeing that I was showing some interest, he offered to play a game. He bet me (with a sly smile on his face) that he could name more names than I could from the biographical section of Webster's. So we began calling off the names of well-known poets—Millay, Pound, Masters, MacLeish, Monroe, Fletcher, and so on. Each of us made a guess as to whether or not it would be present, and then Mr. Frost looked it up. He took a childish pleasure in this, beaming every time he won. I outscored him, however, by the simple method of guessing that older poets would be in and younger poets would not. Finally, he petulantly cried out, "Who decides who shall go in and who shall stay out?"

The first subject he started on was college. He wanted to know my purpose in going back to school, and when I told him it was teaching, he said, "Of course, you are going into English. They usually do. But, do you know, if I were a young man and starting out, I would steer clear of all kinds of English teaching. I would take up some other subject like

Latin or history. That would give me time to devote the most important part of my mind to my work, my writing. Correcting English themes takes too much out of you. I know a lot of men who started out as good writers, and then they were steered out of their writing by their teaching of English and how to write. To my way of thinking, it is all a waste of time anyway. The average student, if he doesn't use the best English in all his courses, undoes the work of his English course. Not many of them do. The other courses demand facts and not good English."

This was the beginning of a long monologue on education. Many times he got off the subject and upon something entirely different. But he would pull himself back to it. He seemed much moved by the thought that here was someone about to embark upon a teaching career, obviously bound for all the pitfalls along the way that Mr. Frost had hit. He wanted to give me the benefit of his experience. He compared colleges. He talked about the "Old Guard" and their jealousies, the faculty members most firmly rooted in their particular school. He discussed teaching and marking methods and recalled incidents of pettiness and squelching of originality. He saw some hope for the future, but present systems appeared pretty dark. "From the time I started teaching," he said, "I would find myself belabored by forces trying to destroy me. What was the use of teaching English anyway? Who would thank you for your pains and sacrifice? For a creative writer, it would be the hardest kind of row to hoe. If I had to teach, a good high school would be better than college, and some subject other than English would be best."

It was plain to see that certain aspects of the educational systems nettled him. To bolster all this talk of the dangers of teaching, he recalled many stories and poems. There was no lessening of his ability to draw richly from the reservoir of his mind, no weakening of his tremendous memory.

When I inquired about Lesley Frost, he spoke a bit about her family and recalled a story which amused him. "I have always admired the independence of that family. They ask nothing of no one. They even won't pay any attention to what I say, even though I know all about trains and schedules; and they won't give me any credit for that. Take my granddaughter, Lee. She called me up long distance from Putney, Vermont, saying that she would arrive at seven in the evening for a short visit with me. Well, I delayed my supper. I ate my supper alone and wondered where she could be. Around ten o'clock the bell rang. It was not Lee but her sister, my other granddaughter, with a boy friend in tow. They were on a scavenger hunt. It seems they had been sent out from their school with a list of things to procure, ridiculous things for which they had to scour Boston. It seems it would take them most of the night. Finally I said, 'Have you heard anything about the whereabouts of Lee?' 'Oh, yes,' was the answer. 'She arrived all right, and now she is out on the scavenger hunt, too.' With that, they were off. Well, I waited up late. At one o'clock in the morning, I took a walk around the block with my dog. No Lee in sight. She's only fifteen, you know. I have never been in the habit of worrying about any of the family. They have always done pretty much as they pleased. I turned in and went to sleep. At about eight in the morning I heard a sleepy voice from a downstairs bedroom yell up to me that the telephone was ringing. I answered the phone and returned to bed. When I finally got up, I found that Lee had risen before me and had gone out, for breakfast probably. She didn't return. Remember, I hadn't seen her yet. At last that night I had a call from the railroad station. She was on her way home, and she was very sorry she hadn't had a chance to see me. But at least she had slept in my house. Do you know, some mothers would have been dreadfully worried about all that gallivanting around on her part. But I guess

I don't make a very good mother or grandmother. Never have."

Noting my interest in American history, he told me that this was one of the best fields for research. His friend Bernard de Voto did it on a grand scale—American lore. There were multitudes of stories scattered about the country. He told me a few—the Vermont man who went to Russia to present an acorn to the Czar; the freethinker who went to Dartmouth, tried to inspire an interest in playacting, and failing, packed all his equipment in a hollow tree and floated down the river with it to new adventures and success. (There is a monument to him at Dartmouth.) Mr. Frost said that countless books could be written about the lore of these states. Many of his friends were sending him little items of interest—stories, pamphlets, books. He had been collecting them to some extent. I thought I detected a wistful desire to write a long book of prose. So I asked him, "Have you ever written a novel, Mr. Frost?"

"I started one once," he said. "But I only completed half a chapter. I was tempted always to run off into verse. So I gave it up."

Getting back to colleges he said, "Colleges are much the same. But teachers are different. If you are lucky, you might get a good one. In my college days I once went to the dean to see about getting a special course under a man who had done some poetry-writing and who sounded interesting. The dean said, 'Just what are your pretensions?' I replied that I was much interested in writing and that I had had a few things published in newspapers here and there. 'Oh, we're a writer, are we?' he said. When he made that comment, I walked out without another word."

When I inquired about David Morton* and his work at Amherst, Mr. Frost told me that Amherst was not any too anxious to have Morton in the first place. The president had

* (1886-1957) Poet and teacher for many years at Amherst.

come to Mr. Frost and had asked him an opinion of this man. The only thing known at the time was that Morton had won a prize for a poem about "Ships" and that the Morrows were strongly for him. Through the influence of Mrs. Dwight Morrow and over the protest of the president, Mr. Morton was taken on. But he was never too popular with the rest of the faculty. For one thing, he had a fight with a policeman, spent a night in jail, and had to be reprimanded by the president. Then again, he developed a habit of dismissing a class after ten minutes if the mood impelled him; the disturbance the students made in leaving the building was disrupting to other classes. Morton was big and handsome and easygoing and harmless—but he did not have a very easy life. His poetry, Mr. Frost thought, was "pretty." The poems were little sketches of flowers and seasons and things, but they contained no great amount of depth.

I asked him about his own work. He said it was about the same from year to year, a certain quantity and no more. He was having a new book in the spring. He had always continued writing, no matter what happened. Some poets had a rough time of it and gave it up. He said, "Take Louis Untermeyer, for instance. I doubt if you'll see any more poems from him. He is doing prose and more anthologies."

College teaching was brought up again when he mentioned Robert Hillyer. When the latter finally left his famous job at Harvard, the president said that that was the last time a poet would mix writing and teaching in that school.

What disturbed him a great deal in college was the marking. It was easy to give the student a double A or a failure. But the intervening marks like B, C, and D were hard to decide. When he was given a job at Pinkerton Academy, he tried the experiment of giving a student a mark on the first day and saying to him, "That will be your term mark. Now if you think you are any better than that, I am willing to be convinced. Come in at any time and convince me. I will change it if you do." One of his teacher friends got into the habit of giving the same grades that a certain lady teacher gave the same pupils. This happened no matter what they did. One pupil wrote the Lord's Prayer backwards and handed it in as an assignment. His mark was a B.

Mr. Frost contended that it was not hard to get a doctor of philosophy degree. Some very unintelligent people have them. One particular friend of his, whose talk borders on the foolish, got one. He knew very little, although he was able to do some surprising things on paper. Mr. Frost remembered how one day this friend came to him in Vermont, walking. No one had given him a ride because he looked so odd, and he was on his way to New York. Mr. Frost cleaned him up, threw his hat away, and made a little pack for his back. "Now," he said, "you will get a ride, I am willing to wager." He was right. The man wrote later from New York, thanking him for what he had done.

He asked me if I could quote any poetry. I said, very little. He wondered that this seemed an art not too common in the race. At least, the colleges were not turning out men who had great memories. And yet, in the old days, it was much more common, particularly among mathematicians. It was not hard to memorize a poem, especially if it had a swing to it. He himself could quote very little free verse, but some singsong ballads he had inadvertently memorized with little effort. To prove it, he quoted several, the first concerning a mermaid and the lighthouse keeper.

He stopped for a while to autograph my books. During this task, his face became relaxed and thoughtful; he had a most gentle look to his features. He labored over the books very carefully, writing from memory. (He wrote out poems in each book.) Once he stopped to ask me how to spell "balance."

I asked how they would allow him to keep on teaching at his age. He said that the president of Dartmouth had once spoken to him about it. Mr. Frost was beyond the age of retirement already. The other teachers were being shunted off at 65, and they looked askance at Mr. Frost. "How old are you?" asked the president. "No one knows exactly," said Mr. Frost. "Well, we'll take that for an answer. We're not sure that you're old enough to be retired."

Note-taking in college was a special peeve of his. He told me the story of his first lecture at Columbia—how he had found himself in a pit, looking up to tiers of seats. All he saw above him were notebooks. So he began by crying out, "Put them away!" No one knew what he was talking about. He had to repeat his outburst. "Put them away! I am not going to say anything worth taking notes on." Finally they did so dubiously. But he saw a few of them try to sneak in a few notes. Note-taking was a bad college habit. He had taught Lesley not to take them. Once this had gotten her into a little trouble with an instructor who thought she was not interested in the course and, moreover, was setting a bad example for the rest of the class. Later, he called to her from across the street, when she was walking with her father, "You surprise me, Miss Frost. You got a B."

Boyishly he picked up some of the Christmas cards and showed them to me. "Here is one that I like especially. It shows the crest of the wave perfectly. It proves what can be done with woodcutting."

When I was ready to leave, he gave me some parting words of advice. "When you go to teaching, don't take it too seriously. Too many people are schoolmarmish. They live only to thrust an education down your throat. There is more to life than just that."

As I walked out into the cold night, I wondered if I would ever see him again. He stood in the doorway for a minute and called to me to be careful of the slippery steps.

I saw Mr. Frost again in September of 1947 at the Albany Institute of Arts and Letters, when I took time out from my studies at Union College to go to his lecture with the hope of shaking his hand again. As it turned out, I had no opportunity to greet him or to exchange a friendly word. I saw him from a distance, over waves of interested people. In the informality of his utterance, however, I found it not impossible to imagine him in the quiet of his Cambridge study, among the tall bookcases. Anxious to see if there was any marked change in Mr. Frost, I sat close to the front of the throng that filled the hall of the Institute. When he came slowly in, preceded by the man who was to introduce him, I looked at his face and did feel that he had changed to some extent. Compared to the time I had last seen him, he appeared much more careworn, tired-looking, aged. He was under the burden of a heavy cold, and it was evident he wanted to get the lecture over and done with as soon as possible. The same massive form was there, the same white hair, the indomitable spirit. Certainly here was no retreat before the flailings of old age. He advanced to speak and he said his words strongly.

A friend with me who had never heard Robert Frost before said of him: "His sincerity breathed out of him with every word and moment that passed."

During the lecture, several unexpected happenings took place. He had always had an excellent memory for poems. On this night, however, he suffered a lapse of memory. In quoting "Birches" he paused for several moments, trying to recall a line. "I guess I know it too well," he said.

Later in the evening he became irked at his audience when they laughed in the wrong places. In his reading of the "Witch of Coos," he amused them by his dialect. At the first laugh he said sternly, "Quiet, please. This is serious." When the laughter broke out again, he said, "Please stop. There is much to read and you make me stop."

A little habit he had developed was to rub his nose as he talked. This bothered a few people.

His reading of poetry, in spite of the occasional lapses, was excellent. I remember that he read "Stopping by Woods on a Snowy Evening" at a much slower rate than formerly. In previous readings, he had spilled out most of it almost in a breath. Now he tried to emphasize the best in each line.

In spite of the few little weaknesses caused by his advancing years, he showed many of the traits that I remembered and loved. The half-serious look and twinkle in his eyes were there; his talk was full of little asides that were almost murmurs but which were caught and appreciated by his audience. He was enjoying himself. When the steam pipes began to snap and competed with his speaking, he stopped to beat time with his hand. He shied away from applause by speaking very quickly after each poem was read.

Later, I asked my friend for his impressions. I was curious to learn how a complete stranger to the Frostian style and treatment would react. He said, "He looked like a fine old gentleman. I had the impression that what he said was not what he thought this night or this week; it was the outcome of a lifetime of belief and ideas about poetry."

I asked my friend what he thought of his voice and manner of speaking. He thought the high-pitched tone he had was individual, rich in accent, not rapid or unpleasant. He had a laugh that came from deep down in him, so sound and jolly that it vibrated in you, too, and made you feel better afterwards. His was a ready mind, a simple but direct speech. One knew that he stood on firm ground. My friend commented that he had "no logical sequence about his reading or his ideas. This, I think, is illustrative of the creative talent. Ideas seem to spring out of him. When he expressed an idea which was his own dictum of poetic theory, I was not bothered by any doubts. He practices what he preaches. He isn't quite conscious of his own powers."

Mr. Frost gave a noteworthy lecture that evening. Here is an excerpt from it, an idea which he apparently had been mulling over:

"I have been wondering lately who really has the best right to poetry—the man who writes it, the man who reads it, or the man who studies it. So many of us get through high school and then through college nowadays that there is great danger that the ones who study it may be in the majority. It is one step from drama. Does the play belong to the person who writes it or the person who acts it or to the person who goes to see it? It doesn't belong very much to the student who studies it. I have just been seeing students and teachers at the Massachusetts Institute of Technology, and I had the feeling that I was with people who would never study poetry. This made me feel very much at home. They haven't time. They are fortunate on looking at poetry just as looking at a play—merely entertainment."

In connection with this, he took a stab at teachers and what they do to poetry:

"You can always get a laugh out of teachers by saying that teachers can get more out of a piece of writing than the writer puts into it. The teacher sometimes squeezes it into worse words. I don't mind anybody who makes more out of one of my poems. Once in a while, I hear of a new way of taking a poem of mine and turning it into ugliness. This is what I call 'disgusting.' . . . You can make play with all sorts of things. I have done it many times. I have not suffered usually; I have been amused usually by the meanings that people give to my poems. You read it many times and it becomes different to you. A smile goes over your mind."

To him, there was a great difference between reading and studying. He let us have the idea in this vein:

"You go to school to learn to read. The further you go, the more you have the attitude that everything is to study. That is the danger. Once a person has learned to read, once he has gotten the flavor of it, he should just let it rest. The annoying thing about this is that many young men feel that poetry is written to be read and studied. If it is written to be studied, I don't see why we don't have it written deeply to be studied."

Near the end of his talk, he gave us a startling simile: "You know, a poem is like a napkin in an old-fashioned napkin ring. The small end is stuck through. You pull it through—and it gets smaller and compressed. All the way through, it suddenly bursts out, opens up."

He followed the talk with a reading of poetry. When he had finished and gone wandering off the stage, he was called back. He put on a show of surprise: "You mean, let them select it?" he said to the man who had introduced him. But it was evident he was too weary to give us many.

After the reading, he hurried down into the audience and was instantly surrounded by a host of admirers hopefully waving books to be autographed. They followed him like buzzing bees into a small anteroom. I gave up the idea of fighting the throng and trying to get near him.

The last I saw of Mr. Frost that evening was his white head borne along as by a wave of people, a murmur of excitement flooding around him. I think Robert Frost liked it. He wanted people to understand, and he must have had the feeling that there were many people in this crowd who understood.

CHAPTER XII

Robert Frost in Vermont—I

FOR THE FIRST TIME, I saw Mr. Frost in his little cabin situated on a hillside in Ripton, Vermont. I took a young friend with me, a college student by the name of Alexander Taylor.* The date was September 1, 1954. We climbed the hill and walked between two stonewalls that led to Mr. Frost's place. The hillside flamed with goldenrod and asters in the September sun. When we approached the top of the hill, it was to look out over a blue swell of mountains, over a landscape that shimmered in the heatwaves. In front of us was a small vegetable garden surrounded by a barbed electrified fence, apparently to keep out trespassing animals. Small cherry trees leaned over in front of the porch. As we walked up the path two small dogs rushed tumultuously to meet us. We heard a vigorous voice in the distance urging them to "hush up!"

I looked carefully at this cabin which served as a summer home for the poet. Its sides were of uneven, unpainted boards, and the porch was sturdy but clumsily put together of wood seemingly picked up haphazardly. The two-by-fours were not all two-by-fours. There were a couple of easy chairs on the porch and some books. When we stepped into the sitting

---

* Now a poet and teacher at the University of Connecticut.

room, we discovered nicely-paneled and varnished walls, easy chairs, and one brand-new chair. There was a small desk with a typewriter on it, some opened letters, postcards, a magnifying glass. Nearby was a bowl of fireweed that had gone to seed; it had become a fluffy, light-brown mass of fibers. A quick glance revealed other objects, including a large built-in bookcase containing about 350 books. (I noted poetry anthologies, the *Dialogues of Plato*, books of criticism on Melville and James, editions of his own works, volumes of Faulkner and Hemingway, and a book on the Mormons.) Next to his chair were manuscripts, books, unopened packages and letters. Beside the biggest chair was a flat, thin board with a propping stick; apparently he used this as a writing desk. There were pictures of birds on the walls, an antique tray on the shelf over the fireplace, a rough drawing of a figure against a sunset, and a large chest in the corner. On the chest lay penciled manuscripts and a book entitled, *Man in the Land.**

Finally, there was Mr. Frost himself, whom I had not seen for a number of years because of academic and other pressures. He was now eighty years old, but for a man of this age he seemed vigorous, well, and not as feeble and aged as some people had described him. He was dressed in blue denim coveralls, a white, frayed shirt, and blue sneakers. His cheeks sagged a little, and his heavy eyebrows jutted out over sunken eyes, but his arms and hands were firm and smooth. As he sat down and began to talk to us, he ruffled his white hair with a hand that trembled just a little bit. But the voice that came from him was strong; the tones were even, melodious, with a slight nasal twang, unchanged from what I remembered over the many years I had known him.

I introduced my friend Sandy Taylor as a budding teacher, and Mr. Frost looked at him with great interest. "You write poetry?" he asked. "Yes," said Sandy. This started him off on

* Published in 1954 by this author, Daniel Smythe.

a train of thought which was a favorite of his—how was the young poet to do his poetry and survive under the pressure of the system? I had heard this before, but it was worth hearing again. He himself had been battling pressures all his life in order to get a body of work done. He saw in Taylor (as he had seen in me) one who was about to start the same road. So we listened to him as he started a long ramble of conjectures and speculations.

"I guess we all have to bow our heads to it, somewhat, for what else is there to do? You can't take up farming, for that's too hard work; and it's just as deadening to get into a publisher's office. Some have tried that. They join a magazine, the *New Yorker*, for example, expecting to do their writing in their spare time. And then they get pressed into the mould just the same; the routine gets them all. College teaching may be the lesser of the evils; but the act of correcting papers is weakening, deadening. It eventually beats you down, defeats you, takes you away from work that is of value. A young poet can be buried and never recover.

"When I started at Pinkerton Academy, I took it seriously at first. But the students threw masses of papers at my head—so I began to see that the system was out to get me. If I were to be a 'good' teacher, I was supposed to do what they told me—but I began to be a poor one. I would have to, in order not to waste valuable time—and it was a waste to go through everything. I got the habit of skimming, of seeing only if the student was bettering or holding his own. I remember one day when the papers struck my desk, I simulated the girl who was buried under the weight of the warrior shields; my knees buckled under the weight of those papers. Then I held them up. 'Does anyone want these papers back?' Nobody did. 'Then they can't be of much value to you,' I said, and dropped them all into the waste basket. They all looked at each other in puzzlement. It wasn't the way a teacher should act. But I did keep tabs on them, told them what marks they were going to get, and urged them to come in and argue it out if they felt they deserved a higher mark.

"As I said, I generally avoided being buried under the shields of that system. I usually changed my place once in a while when I saw that I was beginning to slip under. But young people do get buried. I had a friend who took education seriously. He went to Germany to do graduate work. He came back and took a little country school. He was going to give his students a real education. But shortly after, they made him school superintendent. He couldn't beat the system. They wouldn't let him alone.

"Nothing is so deadening as to have to correct those tiny minor errors. It does no good anyway, for they will make the same errors four years from now. Another deadening thing is the thought that you have to keep piling up knowledge, know more and more about what there is to know. Like that Civil War general, McClellan. He never moved. He was never ready, for he had to have more information about the enemy. He could never get enough to make him go into action, so he had to be removed. I had a good illustration of that recently in a girl who came up from the South. You know, I don't have much to do with this college near here. I have a vague connection that requires very little if anything of me. And that satisfies me. But there is a scholarship, gotten out in memory of my wife. And I pass on some of the applicants. It is a six-weeks' course for which you get college credit. One year, I noticed the name of a girl from a little private school near Atlanta, Georgia. A small, confining, religious place. 'She gets it,' I thought. 'It will give her a little freedom and independence. She will be able to shake off the severe routine and come up here and do nothing but relax.' She came. I didn't see her for five weeks but made an inquiry. They said, 'She may not be doing what you expect of her. She is studying very hard.' After the sixth week, I looked her up. 'How are you doing?' I asked. She smiled happily. 'I took two extra courses.' She must have been surprised by the look on my face. 'Isn't it our duty to know more and more about things?' 'No!' I said. 'Decidedly not!' So she disappointed me. I thought I would get her out into the air, but the system, the nonsense they taught her was too strong....

"Rules . . . they've got it all down in rules, even our own English tongue. Classifications. Specialists in semantics and all that stuff. I don't mind the rules in a foreign language—in Greek, for instance. But not these lists of things in our own tongue. They think everything should be explained. For example, they are still writing books on the reasons for the two world wars. They blame it on something or other and trace it back to Alexander the Great. It's just a part of the system. And another part of it is this Ph.D. business. (I suppose you both are after them.) You have to get one or you don't belong. They look down on you. It's like a union."

Mr. Frost rambled on, sinking down in his chair, rumpling his hair, straying from the point, but always working back to the original point, the deadening effect of educational routine on the creative artist. At one time in the midst of his talking, he got up and drew all the shades and closed the windows because the light bothered his eyes. The room became a little stuffy because it was warm outside, but we did not mind that.

I had heard some criticism of Mr. Frost. A lecturer in Philadelphia declared that he was in his "dotage," that he was losing his memory, that he was fumbling and uneasy and incoherent. These unkindnesses had irked me because they were not true, or so I believed. There was ample evidence of their falsity in what I saw and heard this afternoon. Mr. Frost's memory was excellent. In fact, during the day he quoted verbatim from many sources—the Bible, Homer, Shirley, Ella Wheeler Wilcox, and even from Edgar Guest. His hearing was not as bad as some had painted; I did not have to shout at him. He was full of reminiscences—rich details about his life in England, adventures and talks with Amy Lowell and Ezra Pound, criticisms and estimates of other poets, stories of his teaching and his travels, sharp witticisms. I would only have to mention a college or a person or a book and he would have much to say.

I caught many remarks like these:

"I am not a perfunctory reader of perfunctory writing."

"Today, the poet doesn't eat at the end of the table. He eats under the table."

"I am a writer of books in retrospect."

"No one pushes me into publishing anything, as in the case of E. A. Robinson. They don't dare to bother me."

"A book a year. Robinson buried himself under himself."

> Seven cities claimed Homer dead
> Who when alive refused him bread.

"The neglected poet believes there is a general disregard for poetry. Nobody cares. It has been like that through the ages. You have to rise above it and write as if someone did care."

"Down there in New York, the teachers almost have to wear identification badges to tell them apart."

"Many of the poet-teachers are drifters. Colleges don't hold you if you don't have a Ph.D. Ridiculous situation."

"Amy Lowell told Robinson and myself: 'You don't have a right to write poetry unless you have wealth.' She had wealth, and who the hell is she?"

"Someone said to me the other day, 'There should be an Amy Lowell revival.' If she were alive, she would start one."

"We need less accumulation of knowledge and more action."

"Poetry is a gamble and it is fun. Like this well-driller back of the house. He's had a tough time and has lost money on the deal. He has broken his drills. He told me, 'Drilling is a gamble, and it makes life a lot of fun.' "

As a storyteller Mr. Frost, as usual, was superb. He excelled in telling stories which he had heard from his friends. First, he insisted on telling Taylor a story that I had told him many years ago. It was about an army chaplain who had robbed me of a dozen eggs which I had just liberated from a German family. "One of his atrocity stories," he chuckled.

He told a whole series of stories about "Old Man Smith," a college professor with an original brand of humor, a man who hated both the colleges in his town—the one he worked for and the one at the other end of town. One day he took his family out for a drive in the best car. He promised them a holiday—a rare occasion. But at the first place they stopped in the hills, he discovered (in kicking at the soil) a beautiful boulder. He got the idea that he must have it for a gravestone. So he spent the rest of the day dickering for the sale of the rock and transporting it back home. When Mr. Frost chided him for giving his family such a "holiday," he said, "If I hadn't, Madam Smith would have gotten me a sumptuous stone, and I would have spent eternity turning over and over under it."

He told the story of how Amy Lowell tried to bully him into going to a party; she even told him that he could rehearse with her what he should say. "Nobody tells me what to do or say." So when he met Untermeyer, who was supposed to go to the same party, they made a pact *not* to attend the "damned thing." "Shake," said Untermeyer. Of course, this action aroused the enmity of some of her favorites.

He had a great many stories about Ezra Pound. One was about his "craziness." "I talked with his son, and he sat where you are sitting now. I said, 'Is your father crazy?' He shrugged and said, 'Well . . . you know. . . .' Later, I was talking with T. S. Eliot, and I said to him, 'Is Pound really

crazy?' Eliot also shrugged his shoulders and said, 'Well . . .
you know. . . .' Pound is a stubborn and egotistical man.
Some could make a craziness out of that if they pushed it far
enough."

He told another story. "I remember going to the publisher
Nutt with Pound dressed in those fancy clothes of his and his
cane. He came out with a copy of my first book in print. But
he didn't give it to me. He kept it. I didn't even have a chance
to look at it. Pound reviewed it, but it was such a personal
review that I was ashamed of it and hoped it wouldn't get
around. Many years later I looked it up and found it wasn't so
bad."

He told the story of his daughter and her attendance at a
seminar in literature in which they tore apart poems, comparing the first and final drafts. The poems were by Blake, Yeats,
and Spender. The girl became so disgusted with the class that
she got up and said, "The only poem worth considering is the
one by Blake; the other two are minor poems. Why not just
forget them? And why spoil a poem by comparing all the
drafts? Why not let them alone?" We could see that Mr.
Frost felt she did exactly right.

With a great deal of relish, he told the story of critical
mistakes by two reviewers. One, Ford Madox Ford, believed
that an early work was free verse and said so. However, the
printer had simply left out a word which made the line
swerve from the iambic. "This saved English literature," said
Mr. Frost. Amy Lowell had done much the same when she
mispronounced a word and made it "free verse"—which it
wasn't.

A point that he stressed was the element of luck in poetry
and education. It was luck that got him a house in England
for $50 a year. And it was luck that gained him a full profes-
sorship at Amherst, at the start! He had put the name "Stark"
into a poem in the middle of his volume. It so interested Stark
Young,* whose family name it was, that he pulled a few

* (1881-   ) Author of *So Red the Rose.*

strings and got Mr. Frost appointed to the Amherst faculty as a full professor.

It was luck that brought him fame in America. He took the critics by surprise and sort of bulled his way through. It was better tactics that way. "Go charging through when you see the way," he said. "Luck," he mused, "has a lot to do with acceptances. If a book is sent in at the right time, it might be taken. Sometimes a poetry editor will have had a bad breakfast, or a fight with his wife, or a tough headache—and so you get your poems back. You have to watch for the breaks. What I like is not to be chased for favors. So many chase after me for favors. It's best to go it alone, not even with the gifts of these damned billionaires out in Detroit. Go it alone. You are stronger that way."

He used the word "freedom" a great deal, and stressed independence of thought and action. It was apparently something he had been struggling for all his life. Poets were suspect among college authorities anyway (he quoted again Conant's statement in regard to Hillyer). Poets were harder to press into the mould. Besides stressing freedom of action, Mr. Frost unhesitatingly talked about people and characterized or summarized some of the poets he had known. Many of them had been teachers.

"Robert Coffin," he said, "had a natural gift for poetry. He wrote too much, however, and was sloppy about it, like his classes and his life. He didn't make himself solid as he should have.

"Hillyer let us all down. He had a very important chair, and could have done a great deal. But he drank himself out of it; he fell out of his chair one day. He had been living in a sanatorium anyway, concealing it from everyone. But they caught him.

"Harriet Monroe did a lot for poetry, but she was always looking for favors. (She rejected me once, but she swore she was away from the office at the time.) She hated New

York and did not hide her hate, but she was always going out to push her magazine. She was always looking to me for a boost. A tiny, energetic person, with a touch of TB, but no poet.

"David Morton. An unhappy teacher. He had an unhappy married life. He didn't get along with the authorities and the rules. Eventually he moved to the Canaries.

"Ezra Pound. An eccentric streak in him. He had to be first in everything. He wanted to discover, to break the way—and perhaps that is why he was interested in me.

"Amy Lowell. Just a big noise. She was always kicking up a row somewhere. She once wrote to Jack Squires,* 'I know we are enemies, but let's meet anyway and talk it over.' They met, and he ridiculed the authenticity of her Keats' manuscript. The manuscript was her life, all she lived for. So they had a big row. She had the income from nine million dollars, so she could afford to make a big fuss wherever she went. Everything had to be done over in the hotels where she stopped. The air was full of feathers when they restuffed the pillows."

He had many words for other poets and the writings about them. I gave him some amusement (and perhaps pleasure) when I told him that at least a score of dissertations had been written on Robert Frost. He said, "I am disappointed. Isn't there more than that? Are they any good? Have you read them all?" He maintained that he had not seen one of them.

He brought out some glasses of sarsaparilla as he talked, and we drank that. Here are a few pungent remarks he made about himself, poetry, and audiences:

"The best place to lecture is to the 'town-gown group.' In a small town with a college, you get a mixture of young and old, an educated variety."

"The writing in schools is a dead and frustrating thing."

"Four colleges claim me."

* John Squires (1884-   ) British poet and editor.

[*130*]

"I went to England not to write poetry but to write a novel or a play and to make things right."

"A novel today is written in a publisher's office. The writer brings in an idea, and the editor helps him to throw it together. They rewrite it there."

"Publishing your own work is no good, although some have done it. Robinson and George Meredith did it. The critics look down on a book if it is not by a big publisher. But the stuff never pays. Publishers sometimes publish poetry as a favor to their novelists. They lose money, and they don't want to do it, but it tones up their lists."

He told us the story of how he was investigated at Pinkerton when he tried to beat the system. The state supervisor came in and for two hours watched him conduct classes. "I'm in a fix," Frost thought, "but I might as well go all the way." There were two or three bright students he "could play ball with." They "carried the ball" while the supervisor watched, and no one said a word. Later, he was to hold up Mr. Frost as an example of a good teacher. This man was the type who could pull out his watch at any time of the day and tell you what every teacher in the state was doing.

Mr. Frost picked up the books we had brought and compared the pocket editions carefully. "One of them has sneaked in a lot of advertising on me," he said. Then he autographed them slowly, making comments as he did so.

As parting words of advice, he urged us to "go it alone." He said, "Most people won't leave you alone or help you unbeknown. I did have one friend who helped me and never told me. He was the reviewer who advised Mrs. Nutt to take my first book, and I am sure it was John Drinkwater."*

We took our leave of Robert Frost, our minds ringing with all the words he had spoken to us. As we walked down through the brilliant light of the countryside, Taylor said, "The man is tremendously interesting; he has a brilliant wit and a radiant personality. I shall never forget him."

* (1882-1937)

CHAPTER XIII

Robert Frost in Vermont—II

IN JULY OF 1959, I took my wife Ruth for a visit with Robert Frost in Ripton. I had written beforehand to his secretary for an appointment and was cordially invited.

It was a rainy day, and Mr. Frost had not yet arrived at his cabin, so we turned into the parking lot at the Homer Noble farm and waited. The Noble farm was the home of the poet's secretary, Mrs. Morrison, and her family; their beautiful farmhouse was situated on a hillside many yards below the cabin. Ruth spoke of the cleanliness and freshness of the old place under the rain. The building was surrounded by zinnias and marigolds and there was a heavy grapevine between the house and the garage.

We did not have long to wait, for after a few minutes a car drove up and Mr. Frost got out. He started immediately up the hill path, without looking to the right or the left. We waited for a while before we set out after him.

Following the sturdy stonewall, we went up the path to the cabin. I noted royal ferns and ostrich ferns on the way and there was a small garden near the cabin. We did not have to knock at the door, for his two dogs made such a rumpus that he came out to see what was happening. I introduced him to Ruth, and he welcomed her with a very vigorous hand-shake. He did not seem much changed from when I last saw him, but his stomach seemed a little more pronounced. There was a scar on his nose, so perhaps he had fallen. He asked us to bring in his chair, and when I had done so he slumped down into it and started talking. The cabin interior looked about the same as I had remembered it. I noted the sketches, the piles of manuscripts, the unopened mail, the manuscript notebooks. I glanced quickly at his library shelves—books by Horace, Philip Wylie, Elizabeth Bishop, Plato, Mark Van Doren; and there was the Columbia *Encyclopedia*. Beside him was a calendar appointment list with almost all the spaces filled.

When he began, he mentioned his giving up the job of Library of Congress consultant; a poet by the name of Richard Eberhart was taking his place. He asked if I had ever met Eberhart. When I told him I had not, I added that Untermeyer considered some of his poetry "surrealistic." The word sent Mr. Frost off on a tangent. He recalled the time he had once heard the word "sir" used as a verb. A policeman in London had used it. In speaking of a person, he had said, "You could almost *sir* him but not quite."

When I spoke of Peoria, Illinois, in connection with Bradley University, Mr. Frost said he had once visited this city and had offended an audience there. He had made an inappropriate joke to a club he was addressing. He was making the point that everyone was interested in his own job; no matter how outlandish it was, he felt others should be interested, too. He related that a man who trained dogs to fight each other defended his occupation with the stout assertion, "Why, I even shipped twenty dogs to the Pope of Rome." Mr. Frost had intimated that the Pope was interested in dogfights, and many people in the hall groaned. It seems that there were many Catholics in the audience.

I asked him what it was like in San Francisco when he was young. He said what he remembered most was that his family had had eight addresses in eleven years because his mother was not a good housekeeper. When her home became too grimy or cluttered, his father would take pity on her and take her to a hotel. Then she would take pity on him and ask to go to another house or apartment. Consequently, they were always on the move.

"What were your duties at the Library of Congress, Mr. Frost?" I asked.

"I had no duties. I was supposed to talk with people about poetry, but I remember talking with only three. One was a marine who had written poetry at the South Pole. The most surprising one was a girl who came in weeping. She moved toward me, shouting, 'Well, I am at least better than Edna St. Vincent Millay.' She seemed to have a sense of injustice or something because recognition hadn't come to her."

"Why was she crying?" asked Ruth.

"I don't know exactly, but I might make some guesses. She might have been crying because she was frustrated; or (and here he had a twinkle in his eye) she might have been crying with relief because she had finally gained an audience with me."

I recalled that he had once taught psychology at a teachers' college, but he astonished me by denying the charge. "You will find it in *Who's Who* that way," he said, "but what they did was this: the superintendent of schools brought me in to show the girls that psychology couldn't be used in the class-room. On the first day, I said, 'Let's get rid of the text-book!' So everybody put away the new books and we went to work."

"But you *do* get around a lot, Mr. Frost," I said. "Did you ever get into a situation where you felt you were not wanted?"

"Of course. Once I was invited to a summer boys' camp in Vermont. It was a camp for the upper classes. I gave a little talk to them, and I was impressed immediately by the fact that they were inattentive, not interested. Apparently they had been given a pep talk every day, and I seemed to them only a part of the long, boring program."

"When did you first sell a poem, Mr. Frost?" I asked.

"It was in 1892 when I was at Dartmouth. I saw on the magazine shelves a magazine that contained a long poem by Richard Hovey. It covered the whole front page and part of the second. This was a magazine in newspaper form. I got the idea that I would send a poem to them. They published my poem and they sent a check for twenty dollars. With the check I had this note, 'Please learn to spell the name of our magazine correctly.' "

I mentioned his friend Cornelius Weygandt,* and he became very much interested. "A good man," he said. "He liked to laugh at himself, tell stories about himself. He said that once he chided a student for not attending class. The student said, 'I am taking your course from the floor below!' It was apparent that Dr. Weygandt had a bellowing voice and the student could hear everything.

I mentioned Sidney Cox's book about the poet, *A Swinger of Birches*. Mr. Frost maintained that he was not particularly wild about the book because he had heard it was more about the author than about himself. (He confessed that he had not really read the book carefully.) He felt that the book by Reginald Cook was much better. The trouble with Cox was that he was not really a writer.

"What about your new book, Mr. Frost?"

"What book?"

"I saw it mentioned by John Ciardi in the *Saturday Review*."

"We are not so sure about that. You know, I don't have to write if I don't want to—or publish anything. I write and

---

* (1871-1957) Author and teacher at the University of Pennsylvania for many years.

publish only when it is enjoyable. The next book will eventually come out. But there is no set time as yet."

Then he abruptly changed the subject. He started to talk about prejudice.

"I hate to get into an argument with a prejudiced person. Many people are very vehement, and this vehemence is hatched out of their strong prejudice. After listening for a while, you can see the insanity of what they preach. You get the feeling that they could just as vehemently argue for any kind of belief.

"Did I ever tell you about the 'summer Methodist' we have near here? He is a rabbi, and he comes from Cincinnati, and he preaches in the Methodist church. After listening to one of his sermons, a lady said to me, 'Just what is the difference between him and us?' She was baffled. This rabbi is an interesting man who has a habit of dropping in on me once in a while and discussing religious matters. He knows the New Testament as well as he knows the Old, and he maintains that all the material in the New can be found in the Old. He has intimated that it is foolish and futile for two religions to have differences, since they study the same book.

"Once I preached in a synagogue. I didn't know what I was going to talk about until I was introduced. As I was waiting in my chair, I thumbed through the Jewish Bible and I noted these words, 'You don't say to God, What do you think You are doing?' So I used this as a text and preached a sermon. One of the examples I used was that of a woman whose best friend's child was killed in an accident. She said to me, 'I resent that.' I answered her, 'At whose feet are you going to lay your resentment?' "

Eventually, we turned the conversation to editors and publishers. When I suggested to Mr. Frost that a poet might be helped by another poet, he disagreed.

"I don't believe in that, and I never have. It doesn't help

you to be pushed. After all, the editors are the last word when it comes to publication. Of course, some of them are SOB's. But I must say this: the better publishers don't pay much attention to people who push you, even though the pushers are famous people."

Here he paused and looked at me as if another idea had just struck him.

"I never pushed you, did I?" he said.

"No, Mr. Frost, you never did."

"And it did you good. Just how did you get started?"

"I just sent out my work and waited for an answer."

"And they either accepted you or rejected you! That's the way it should be. Stay clear of help. Do it yourself. It is more important that way."

He spoke of a poet, a former student who wanted advice.

"I advised him strongly not to print his first book. He was not ready for it, and it's a bad thing to disappoint people. But the man was determined to be published; and when the book came out, he didn't speak to me for many years."

Since we did not want to weary him too much (he told us he had had a busy day), we decided to leave. He rambled for a while longer on the word "horology," as he got up with us and followed us to the door. He did not seem to want to let us go without more talk, so he walked a little way on the path with us, talking constantly.

CHAPTER XIV

Robert Frost in Vermont—III

A DIALOGUE which I found particularly impressive was one which took place in Ripton on June 28, 1960. There were to be two more conversations, but this one struck me as the most vivid and revealing.

I entered his small cabin room, and Robert Frost commenced in this way:

"Where have you come from?"

"Silver Lake, New Hampshire."

"Yes, I know that region. It is very nice there. You have a cabin? You can leave things from one year to the next?"

"Yes, but we don't leave very much."

"There are several famous people in that vicinity, aren't there?"

"E. E. Cummings. Samuel McCord Crothers* and J. G. Whittier used to live near there."

"I know Cummings. He's a shy fellow with his head tilted a little as if he had a stiff neck or something. He's a real poet. His poetry is typographically odd sometimes. I don't think that gets him anywhere. But I have talked to him. Do you know him?"

"No, I have never met him. I have waved at him."

"I am still down at Washington a few days a year. It

* (1857-1927) Boston minister, essayist, and author of a 1921 book on Emerson.

doesn't amount to much. I am supposed to be a consultant in poetry, but there is little to do. They have put me across from the AFL-CIO headquarters, and that makes me a little nervous. I said to them, 'Look here, I don't belong to a union. Poetry has no union, but it's organized.' They treat me very well.

"Politics? Kennedy came to see me the other day. It was because in an interview I said that the next President would be from Boston. The papers next day headlined, FROST COMES OUT FOR KENNEDY. I think Kennedy will get it, but he has two difficulties, Khrushchev and the Pope."

"Vermont is Republican."

"But it is swinging toward the Democratic side. There is a great influx of French Canadians in the cities, and these usually vote Democratic."

"Do you think his religion will be a drawback?"

"Not much, today. People are more concerned about Russia than about their candidates."

He thought about this for a while. Finally, I asked, "What do you think of the Beatnik poetry?"

"I've read only Ginsberg's *Howl*. I have it here somewhere. It's not very good—just a pouring out. Anyone can do it."

"Why do W. C. Williams and Marianne Moore go for it?"

"I don't know. It's a disorganized poetry, and I think poems need form. Do they get published?"

"The *Herald-Tribune* gave them a whole page last Sunday."

"Irita Van Doren would do that. She is somewhat radical. And Marianne Moore is a little witch. But I like her. She was from Brooklyn and loved baseball—the Dodgers. They broke her heart when they moved to California."

"Don't you think the Beatnik movement is like the Dada movement in France after World War I?"

"Possibly. A fad. Poetry *should* be without whiskers, I

think. I met one of them at an art exhibit. There was a curly wire of some sort hung from the ceiling, and he called it something. I said, 'Do you like it? What is it you are trying to do with this?' He replied mournfully, 'I want to live in my times.' 'But such things,' I persisted, 'won't last.' 'Nothing ever lasts,' he replied. I shut up after that."

"Your poetry is well organized."

"I try to make good sentences fit the meter. That is important. Good grammar. I don't like to twist the order around in order to fit a form. I try to keep to regular structure and good rhymes. Though I admit that Emily Dickinson, for one, didn't do this always. When she started a poem, it was 'Here I come!' and she came plunging through. The meter and rhyme often had to take care of itself."

"You do have twelve syllables in the first line of *The Death of the Hired Man*."

"I do, and that's a mistake. I should have corrected it."

"What about your development in poetic technique?"

"I had no development. I just gradually grew into the right forms. That is the best way. A writer is in a bad way if he has to take writing courses and learn to write by the book. He should feel his way along by himself and let the technique grow on him. Don't study it. Aim for the proper sentence to meet its grammar in a line."

"Emily Dickinson didn't study technique."

"But she should have been more careful. She was more interested in getting the poem down and writing a new one. I feel that she left some to be revised later, and she never revised them. And those two ladies at Amherst printed a lot of her slipshod work which she might not have liked to see printed. She has all kinds of off rhymes. Some that do not rhyme. Her meter does not always go together."

As examples of this, he quoted from memory a number of stanzas and particular lines. It was clear that he knew much of her poetry by heart—more than I had suspected.

"You don't look jaded," he said. "Do they give you time to write at your university?"

"They are in favor of faculty writing."

"It seems to be the tendency nowadays, much more so than in the earlier years. The teacher is getting more time to do as he pleases, and the student has to take more responsibility, be more on his own. Of course, this is the way they do it on the continent. I remember asking Jack Squires what he did at Oxford. He said, 'Most of the time I played cards.' Once his tutor dropped in and asked him, 'How is it with you, Jack?' 'All right. Are you worried? Should I drop in on a class?' 'Oh, no, no, no! Do it your own way. I just wanted to see if you were satisfied.' But they have it that way in England, and it is tending that way here. Students stay away from classes, and no one says anything. The teacher has more leisure time—and they like him to be busy at other activities. Look at what they have done for me. I am supposed to be at Amherst a month at the end of a year and a month at the beginning of the next; and I have whittled it down to two weeks at each end. They haven't cut the pay. I have been in only three academic processions in my life."

"But this hasn't always been so," I reminded him.

"No. I had to keep running away. I started my first teaching at Pinkerton Academy, and they heaped the work on me. I taught thirty-five hours a week, whereas the teacher with a college degree taught twenty-five. It was so exhausting I was practically in a coma. This hurt my digestion, and I finally quit.

"Then I taught up at Plymouth, the New Hampshire State Normal school. I did well there, so well that they thought of making me head of the school. But I persuaded them it wouldn't look good in the catalog to have a man without a degree. They were naive enough to believe that I might be able to pick up one by doing a little extra work somewhere. But I ran away.

"Then I went to England and came back and was offered a job at Amherst. I didn't have to do too much. But I did have a writing course that embarrassed me, and I was asked to drop in occasionally on the classes of my colleagues. That offended some of them. Others felt obliged to have me.

"I left finally and got along by lecturing and writing for a year or so. Then to Michigan as poet in residence. I did nothing there. Finally, I went back to Amherst for a couple of years and had a couple of seminars at Harvard. I had a session at Dartmouth; and at last I came back to Amherst where I'll always be, I guess. I should retire—we have an understanding about a retirement stipend. But they want me to hang on since they have a new president."

"You will continue with lecturing?"

"Yes, I have thought of just doing that a few times a year. My lectures get me from a small amount (the smallest from the New School) to a thousand dollars. The head of the Young Men's Hebrew Association said she would pay me a thousand if I would settle on one set amount for each lecture. It didn't seem fair to her for me to vary so much. This year she paid me seven fifty, so I guess she knows I haven't varied. Five hundred is probably about the average. I have a policy: if I set the price when they ask me, I stick to it; but if they set the price, I usually take it."

"When you were at Harvard as a student, did they have the daily theme?"

"Yes, they did. I wasn't concerned with that sort of stuff— a theme a day. But I remember the freshmen hurrying across the campus to get their themes in the mail by the nine o'clock deadline. That was the famous English A. However, English A at Harvard has gone out now. At one time Ted Morrison was in charge of it. He had twenty instructors working for him. You had to have an army of people to correct that flood of papers. Now Ted has a better job."

"What do you think of the colored race and its struggle for equality?"

"I am all for it. Understand me, I am on their side. I was glad when Patterson beat the Nordic. It was about time he was beaten. I do feel that they have a serious drawback—but not in all Negroes (I shouldn't generalize); there is sometimes that chip-on-the-shoulder, watching for any suggestion that they are not equal to the white man. Some have an inner disturbance or complex of some sort. It can be embarrassing, and I don't like to be bothered by it, although I have known many colored people and have been friends with them. As I told them down in Washington, I hope they get a chance to do something for themselves here which they were never able to do in Africa. Africa, you know, never contributed anything to the progress of the world—no alphabet, no literature, perhaps just a few primitive pieces of art and music. But I knew Langston Hughes, and I knew James Weldon Johnson very well. He was a splendid fellow. (He didn't have hate for the white race.) He brought himself up from being a newsboy on the streets of Boston and made something of himself. It was a pleasure to talk to him. And then I knew Bunche* and Hastie.** Hastie is an extraordinary man. He was one of my former students, too. I look for him to be a Justice of the Supreme Court some day. The first Negro on the Court. He has done great work wherever he has been."

"Did you know William Braithwaite?"***

"Very well. He is going to get out another one of his anthologies soon. But here is a man who has flaws, although he has never done anything bad to me. Some didn't like him because he was always pleading for help or publicity for his books. He never paid his contributors."

"He was good for poetry?"

* Ralph Bunche (1904-   ) Diplomat and UN Under Secretary for Special Political Affairs.
** William H. Hastie (1904-   ) Federal Judge in Philadelphia.
*** (1878-1962) Poet and anthologist.

"In a way, yes. He had a whole page in the old Boston *Transcript*, and he printed the works and pictures of the poets. What I remember most was that he was very poor in grammar since he had little education. He wrote a novel, and his publisher hired Lesley to straighten out the English before they published it. But I have nothing against him."

He was quiet for a minute and then abruptly changed the subject.

"What is this college you work at?"

"Bradley University."

"Oh, yes. What is your rank there?"

"Assistant Professor."

"That's all right. Are you friendly with the students? Do you have them to your home?"

"We have some of them."

"That is the way."

I prepared to leave, but he seemed reluctant to let me go. He insisted on walking with me down the path between the walls, and he walked slowly as his dog raced around us. As he walked, he pummeled me with more questions. Had I noticed the birds and flowers around his place? How was I going to get back to Silver Lake? What had happened to the Christmans and their farm? Who was at the farm? Did I know that Whitman had been discovered by the French? How many hours did I teach at Bradley and what courses? Did I know any Latin? How was I able to get around so much in the summer time? Did I notice how he liked to "snap the quip" in his poetry? Did I know that MacLeish was at Harvard, teaching students to write verse plays?

We came to the end of the path. He shook hands and said, "This is as far as I'll go with you. Good luck. Drop in on me now and then. I like to hear from you. Remember me to all."

He turned around and started the slow walk back to the cabin.

CHAPTER XV

The Last Ripton Visits

O N AUGUST 8, 1961, I paid a visit to Robert Frost, in the company of my wife Ruth. We met him in his little cabin in Ripton and noted immediately a transformation. He seemed much feebler, with his lame knee and watery eyes; his voice quavered at first but it grew stronger as he talked. He wore bedroom slippers, socks, a longsleeved shirt, and yellow pants.

He may have appeared feeble, but there was nothing wrong with his memory or curiosity. In the course of our long talk, he mentioned or discussed thirty-nine different people, including Robinson, Truman, Roosevelt, Meiklejohn of Amherst, Chief Justice Warren, and E. E. Cummings.

His first words to us were, "Tell me where you have come from and what you have been doing." He grew more animated against the background of books, the new editions to be autographed, the flood of manuscripts on the table, the fireplace and the comfortable rocking chairs. There was a bowl of Queen Anne's lace and a single rose on the table.

Here are some of the highlights of his conversation:

He recalled a chat with Harry Truman, who, he said, talked always as if he were reciting a speech in school. (Mr. Frost did an imitation.) Mr. Frost told him that at the Battle of Gettysburg, Lee and Meade were confused and troubled; the only man who knew what it was all about was a man named Hancock, a Democrat who later ran against Garfield for President. Mr. Frost told him a real history of the Civil War should be written. Harry Truman said, "Well, I'm going to write it." Mr. Frost replied, "You'd better hurry up or I'll beat you to it." When he said he favored Hancock over Garfield for President, Mr. Truman said, "Hancock's trouble was he was too fat."

He spoke of the Christman Sanctuary and told again his stories of the place. He said they had treated me very well and had provided a very good home for me. He asked about Lansing* and said, "Give him my regards." He wondered what Henry* and Zoe were doing. Musingly, he went over the place, the creek, the fields, the birds he saw there; he pondered the nature enthusiasts who lived in the vicinity, their knowledge of birds and flowers. "What did W. W. Christman die of? How old was he?" When I told him, he exclaimed, "Such a young man!" (W. W. was 72.) He inquired how I got in touch with this family, and when I told him about *Trails,*** he talked a little bit about Fred Lape.

He recalled my war manuscript and thought it should have been stronger; it didn't contain the horror of war or any atrocity stories. Then he said to Ruth, "Do I dare to tell you one he told me?" I said, uneasily, "Go ahead." He repeated a story I told him many years ago, about the officer who was insulted by German SS prisoners, men I shortly thereafter helped to bury. He said there were rough times in the war, but people were like that everywhere. He maintained that he would hate to be a criminal and be arrested by his neighbors and taken to jail. On the way, he might be given a good going over by these Americans.

I inquired whether a publisher had ever asked him to leave out a poem. "An English publisher did once," he said. "It was the four-line poem about the atom bomb which I meant as sarcasm. We invented the bomb and then said it's no fair to

* The sons of W. W. Christman.
** Nature magazine edited by Fred Lape. See Introduction.

[*146*]

use it any more. The English thought it was a twit against them. They were sensitive about it.

"We have made many mistakes," he added. "We shouldn't have dropped the bomb. We had the war won anyway, but the order was given. Truman was a fool. He made drastic errors, and all the Korean mess shouldn't have been. The recall of MacArthur was one. MacArthur had the Chinese where he wanted them, and a few bombers would have settled their hash, but he wasn't allowed to. I think the politicians were believing that MacArthur was getting too strong, that he might want to be President some day. It was the playing of politics (my opinion). That Berlin business, too, was a big mistake, like the Danzig Corridor. Here we are with Communist territory all around us. That should never have been. That is why Khrushchev can rant and threaten against us. There is always trouble when countries get that close together. That 'peace and good will toward men' is a lot of nonsense. The Poles and the Germans at Danzig—there was always trouble between them. Danzig was Poland's only access to the sea."

He went on like this for some time and then talked of terrible things in our own country, the John Birch Society, for example. "Did you hear how they have offered a prize for an essay on the impeachment of Warren of the Supreme Court? It is defamation of character, and I don't see why he can't sue or something. There must be some protection against this sort of thing. There are bad eggs around everywhere, even on college faculties. I was talking with Philip Wylie, and Phil said, 'There must be a better race of beings somewhere in the universe; that's the only thing that keeps me going, the hope that there may be better people.' But I doubt it. Look at the Communists! Even Rockwell Kent* has gone over to Russia, giving all his paintings to Moscow. Look at Conant shaking his hands in glee when the first bomb was

* (1882-   ) Artist and former president of the Artist's League of America.

[147]

exploded! He should have been awe-stricken, not exultant. He should not have laughed over it. On every college faculty there are squabbles and jealousies. Professors will often attack the president, especially if he has not given their departments enough credit. And they always follow up their accusations that he is incompetent by asserting he is a 'liar' also. You will note that college presidents usually last about four years. I had a good one at Michigan. But he talked too much; he was a little leftish and radical, especially about birth control. He was a scientist and had thousands of mice on which he experimented. Once I suggested to my students that we should put a banner over the campus on which was written in large letters, MORE MICE AND LESS MEN. It is surprising that intelligent men have such hate for each other. I meet with it everywhere."

I asked him about his trip to Jerusalem. He said that he flew there and to Athens and that it was like any other lecture tour he had had. Practically everyone spoke English—and he had had large audiences. (This had not been the case in South America, where so many spoke Portuguese that he had wondered if they knew what he was talking about.) There was lots of activity, lots of money in Israel. They had a million dollar hospital given them. Everyone was interested in something, had something to do. But there were barbed wires between them and Jordan, and every now and then someone on one side would take a pot shot at the other.

"I didn't like South America," he said. "But I do remember flying over the mountains and looking down on the town where Harriet Monroe was buried. Did you ever have any dealings with her?"

"Yes. I had some correspondence with her many years ago about some poems in *Poetry*."

"How did she treat you?"

"Rather snappily at times."

"She was a snappy person. She was not a very good poet, and yet she wanted to be a great one. Once she asked me to get her a reading at Amherst. After that episode she got furious with me, and we remained 'friendly enemies.' You see, I was not teaching a class at Amherst at the time, so I could not order my students to attend. It was not a large audience, and she considered it a failure. She never forgave me because I did not do more."

He spoke of many other people that day, including his children and grandchildren. He spoke of death once. His illustrator was dead and had died a hard death. Mr. Frost said, "His last words to me were, 'Well, Robert, we've put on a good show.'"

When we came to leave, he shook hands with us warmly and urged us to send him some poems and come back and see him again. He did not follow us down the path this time.

We were to see him once more, on August 2, 1962, just a short while before he left for his trip to Russia. When we walked up the winding path in the warm summer sun, we did not think for a moment that this would be our final visit to the place and its occupant.

We knocked on the door of the little cabin, and he welcomed us in. Apparently he had been resting on his bed, for his white shirt and blue-serge pants were wrinkled. He tried to straighten up his clothes a little as he ushered us into the sitting room.

"You must excuse me," he said. "I have just had a trying day. I have just been over to Hanover where I autographed one thousand copies of my new book."

When we exclaimed over this surprising feat, he talked a bit about the problems of autographing. He felt there was no pleasure in signing one's name a thousand times, and it was a chore he would not care to repeat. Because of the pressure of time, he was not able to write anything in the books except his name. It was a very impersonal job, but a necessary one.

"But this is nothing," he said. "Recently, in Florida, they sent a man down with 1500 copies to sign. I didn't think I could do it, and I told him so. They sent merely the unbound sheets of the deluxe edition, and I went ahead and signed them, a hard bit of work. The object was to make a little money. We have to make a living."

He went into some detail about this publisher's agent and the difficulty they had in getting the signature down on so many loose-leaf copies. But finally it was all over, and after the man was gone, Mr. Frost took off a few days to rest his arm and recover.

He rocked contentedly in his rocker for a while. Ruth said, "Do you call that a Kennedy rocker?" "No," he said. "This is a Vermont rocker."

He did not impress me as very much changed from a year ago. If anything, he seemed a little stronger and younger. He hinted that he was a trifle tired, but his subsequent actions in his potato patch did not support this.

I reminded him that John Holmes was dead.

"Yes," he said. "It is a great tragedy. And such a young man. He was always a good friend. Didn't I meet you first at Tufts with John and Raymond Holden?" I nodded. "It was such a sudden illness. For one while he seemed all right, and then he was gone."

The mention of Holden reminded him that Raymond had recently visited him in the company of Henry and Zoe Christman. They had had a good talk. He described in detail some of this conversation and how glad he had been to see them.

As he talked, a small kitten walked into the room and jumped up into his lap. When I suggested that I take a photograph, he said, "Don't take my picture with the kitty! It's not mine."

[*150*]

I spoke of Jerry Brace* at Deer Isle, Maine, and he was instantly very much interested. He asked me several quick questions about Jerry: what he was doing, what type of place he had at Deer Isle, and what he looked like at the present time. He recalled the days when Jerry was in his classes at Amherst.

He said suddenly, "By the way, what denomination are you?" I said, "I am a Unitarian, and Ruth is a Quaker." He said, "They are both just as bad. In fact, the Unitarians are getting worse because now they are trying to drag God into the picture."

"They are doing too much for humanity," grumbled Mr. Frost. "In a way it is interfering with God. Now take electronics. That's a big field."

He asked me if I ever got back to New Hampshire. I said that in the summer I visited relatives in Haverhill, Massachusetts, and passed through New Hampshire. He said, "I know all that section very well—Haverhill and Plaistow. That used to be my stamping grounds before I came to Vermont."

I spoke of his friends, the Christmans, and he was again alert instantly. He threw a lot of questions at us about the Christman farm, and he asked about the son and heir and what he was doing. I described Lansing as best I could and drew a picture of the wild-life sanctuary. Many of his questions were the same that he asked in other years; he recalled at some length his long-ago visit there.

We spoke of his last book, and he admitted it was fourteen years between this book and the one before. I mentioned the trouble we had in getting copies. "There shouldn't be trouble," he said. "If a bookstore tells you, 'We don't have the book in stock but we'll order,' you should never go back there. They are not much good."

He asked for our books to autograph, and when I suggested

* Gerald Brace (1901-   ) Novelist, teacher at Boston University, and former pupil of Robert Frost.

some inside pictures, he said, "No, let's wait until we get outside, and then you can take all you want. I am going to have to dig some potatoes."

After the autographing, we went outdoors. He found a pail, a hoe, and a shovel, and with them he hurried down to the garden. I offered to carry some of these, but he said, "No, I'll do it."

We had a perfect day against the background of the Vermont mountains. In the middle of all of it, Mr. Frost walked securely down the pathway. He headed for his garden patch, and this was a wild one. There were potato vines, string beans, and corn here and there. Everything seemed to have been done to conserve space, but the growth was tremendous. Into this jungle marched Mr. Frost, and in a short while he was raking potatoes into his pail with great gusto.

He refused all our offers to help him. "Shucks!" he said, when he cut a potato in half. "I hurt that one!" He did not seem anxious to talk as he worked. Ruth helped him pick up some of the potatoes while I took pictures, and he appeared very intent on this work. I was surprised that a man of eighty-eight could be so energetic. Finally, he started back to the cabin with his pail half-filled with potatoes. Somehow, through this little episode, his independence had been once more asserted.

We followed him back to the cabin and then took our leave. As we shook hands, Ruth came close and kissed him on the cheek. I think this startled him, and he became a little emotional. His face twisted a little bit on one side, and he talked hurriedly like this: "Send me your books when you get them finished. Write to me. You know I don't write letters. There are too many of them. But I like to hear. Don't forget me. Good-bye . . . Good-bye . . . Good-bye. . . ." And his voice trailed off to a whisper.

That was the last we ever saw of him.

Index

Index

Abercrombie, Lascelles, 20
Adams House, 69
Albany Institute of Arts and Letters, 117
Alexander the Great, 125
Allen, Hervey, 15, 46, 61, 101
American Academy of Arts and Letters, 12
American Mercury, 107
American Song, 61
America Was Promises, 97
Amherst College, 21, 22, 83, 113, 128
Anthology of American Poetry, 12
Aristotle, 84
Atkinson, N. H., 35
Atlantic Monthly, 31, 54, 55, 61

Bible, The, 125, 136
"Birches," 29, 32, 37, 55, 117
Bishop, Elizabeth, 133
Blake, William, 128
Blanchard, Harold H., 48
Bogan, Louise, 52
Boie, Mildred, 62
Boston *Evening Transcript*, 144
Boston *Globe*, 60
Boy's Will, A, 11, 20, 22, 23, 64
Brace, Gerald, 151
Bradley University, 133, 144
Braithwaite, William S., 143
Bread Loaf, 22, 66, 74, 108
Brooks, Van Wyck, 55
Bruce, Ed, 96
Bryant, William Cullen, 17

Bunche, Ralph, 143
Burns, Robert, 72, 74

Cardin, Charles, 104, 105
Cather, Willa, 71
Century Magazine, 83
Chamberlain, Neville, 107
Christman, Henry, 13, 146, 150
Christman, Lansing, 13, 151
Christman, W. W., 13, 63, 91, 146
Christman, Zoe, 146, 150
Christman Wildlife Sanctuary, 13, 144, 151
Ciardi, John, 135
Civil War, The, 107
Cleghorn, Sarah, 100
Coffin, Robert P. Tristram, 66, 107, 129, 130
Columbia *Encyclopedia*, 133
Collected Poems, 11, 22, 45
Complete Poems, 86
Conant, James B., 147
Cook, Reginald, 135
Cox, Sidney, 135
Crothers, Samuel McCord, 138
Cuba, 46
Cummings, E. E., 138, 145

Danzig Corridor, 147
Dartmouth, 81, 108
"Death of the Hired Man, The," 21, 140
Deer Isle, Maine, 151
Derry, N. H., 12

De Voto, Bernard, 42, 113
Dickinson, Emily, 91, 140
Dobie, Frank, 58
Doughty, Rev. John, 16
Drinkwater, John, 131
"Dust of Snow," 57

Eberhart, Richard, 133
Einstein, Albert, 75
Eliot, T. S., 75, 127, 128
Emerson, Ralph Waldo, 15, 80, 85
Endymion, 65
England, 11, 20, 24, 83, 104
Engle, Paul, 46, 61

Faulkner, William, 122
Finnegans Wake, 74
"Fire and Ice," 52
Fisher, Dorothy Canfield, 100
Fletcher, John Gould, 86, 110
Ford, Ford Madox, 128
Frost, Belle Moody (Mother), 16, 17
Frost, Carol, 23, 59, 62
Frost, Elinor (Wife), 18, 19, 22
Frost, Eliot (Son), 22
Frost, Irma (Daughter), 23
Frost, Lee, 112
Frost, Lesley, 23, 92, 93, 94, 96, 97, 102, 112, 116
Frost, Marjorie (Daughter), 22
Frost, Robert Lee
    Advice on colleges, 84-85
    A friend's reaction to, 118
    As a tramp, 48
    At home, 78, 88, 102
    Atom bomb, opinion of, 146-147
    Autographing, 150, 152
    Beatnik poetry, 139
    Birds, 51
    Calypso Orchis, 81
    Common man, 100
    Cooking, 89
    Digging potatoes, 152
    Early youth, 18
    Editors, 131
    Education, 111
    Finances, 82
    First poem, 17, 104
    Friend's reactions, 118

Grading, 114, 123
Honorary degrees, 24
Indifference to landscape, 48
In England, 83
Israel, 148
Jerusalem, 148
Jordan, 148
Key West, 73
Lecturing, 28, 29, 32
Library, 122, 133
Nature, 51, 81
Negroes, 94, 143
Note taking, 116
Opinion of publishers, 89
Opinions of poems, 79
Phrenology, 106
Poetry publication, 22-23
Poetry societies, 91-92
Politics, 139
Quakers, 98, 151
Religion, 42, 84-85, 98-99, 108, 136
Reviews, 64, 65, 66
Stories, 100-101
Story of his life, 82
Students and Mr. Frost, 69, 71, 76, 88, 123
Teaching, 82, 111, 116, 123
Trip to Russia, 12, 149
University of Michigan, 21, 142
Use of his poems by others, 37
Vanity publishing, 50
Versification, 79, 80, 85, 86
War, 101, 102, 103
Writing poetry, 58, 79, 80, 81, 90, 105
Young children writing, 54
Frost, William Prescott (Father), 16

Garfield, James A., 145
Garnett, Edward, 31
Gibbs, Josiah Willard, 75
Gibson, Wilfrid, 20
Ginsberg's Howl, 139
Guest, Edgar, 125

Hancock, Winfield, 145
Harper's, 14
Harvard Lectures, 27, 67, 69, 83, 142
Harvard Poetry Forum, 14

Harvard University, 9, 19, 21, 22, 23, 27, 67, 69, 81, 83, 142, 144
Hastie, William H., 143
"Haunted Palace," 38
Hemingway, Ernest, 122
Hillyer, Robert, 66, 75, 86, 114, 129
Holden, Raymond, 34, 150
Holden, Richard, 34
Holmes, John, 14, 34, 37, 55, 94, 150
Homer, 125
Homer Noble Farm, 132
Horace, 133
House of Representatives, 12
Hovey, Richard, 135
Hughes, Langston, 143
Hulme, T. E., 75

Independent, The, 17, 19
International Writers' Congress, 24
In The Clearing, 24
Ipswich, 55

Jeffers, Robinson, 61
Job, 99
John Birch Society, 147
Johnson, James Weldon, 143
Joyce, James, 74

Keats, John, 17, 62, 65
Keats' Manuscript, 130
Kennedy, John F., 24, 139
Kent, Rockwell, 147
Khruschchev, Nikita, 139
Korea, 147

Lamia, 65
Landis, James M., 96
Landor, W. S., 80
Lankes, J. J., 45, 149
Lape, Fred, 13, 146
"Last Haying," 90
Lawrence, Mass., 17, 19, 31
Lee, General Robert E., 17, 145
Lewis, John L., 71
Library of Congress, 24, 133, 134
Lincoln, Abraham, 107
Lindsay, Vachel, 95
Lord's Prayer, The, 115
Louis, Joe, 96

"Lovely Shall be Choosers, The," 39
Lowell, Amy, 72, 127, 128, 130

MacArthur, Douglas, 147
MacDowell Colony, 66
MacLeish, Archibald, 32, 41, 53, 97, 110, 144
Malam, Charles, 47
Man in the Land, 122
March, John Monchure, 50
Markham, Edward, 79
Masque of Mercy, A, 94
Masque of Reason, A, 94
Masters, Edgar Lee, 12, 110
McClellan, General George, 124
Meade, George, 145
Meiklejohn, Alexander, 21, 145
Melville, Herman, 122
"Mending Wall," 29
Meredith, George, 131
Millay, Edna St. Vincent, 54, 110
Milton, John, 17
Monroe, Harriet, 83, 104, 110, 129, 148
Moore, Marianne, 139
Moore, Merrill, 66
Mormons, 122
Morrison, Mrs. Theodore, 60, 61, 62, 132
Morrison, Theodore, 142
Morton, David, 113, 130
Mountain Interval, 64
Munro, Harold, 20

New Hampshire State Normal School, 141
New Yorker, 123
New York Herald Tribune, 60, 139
North of Boston, 12, 13, 21, 75
Nutt, Mrs. Howard, 20, 131

O'Connell, Cardinal, 95

Paradise Lost, 105
Patterson, Floyd, 143
Peoria, Illinois, 133
Pershing, John, 71
Phi Beta Kappa, 12, 34, 54
Pinkerton Academy, 19, 53, 105, 114, 123, 130, 141

Plaistow, N. H., 35, 51, 151
Plato, 122, 133
Poe, Edgar Allan, 17, 38
Poetry, 41, 83, 104, 148
Portsmouth, N. H., 73
Pound, Ezra, 20, 79, 83, 110, 127, 128, 130
Pulitzer Prizes, 12, 22, 23

Quarterly Review, 65

Ralph Waldo Emerson Fellowship of Poetry, 23
Rhodes Scholars, 46, 47
Rice, Cale Young, 41
Ripton, Vermont, 121, 132, 138, 145
Rittenhouse, Jessie, 30
Robinson, Edwin Arlington, 95, 126, 145
Roosevelt, Franklin D., 97, 145
Root, E. Merrill, 50
"Runaway, The," 29

Salem, New Hampshire, 67
Sandburg, Carl, 75, 95
San Francisco, Calif., 16, 17, 95
San Francisco *Bulletin*, 17
Sao Paulo, Brazil, 23
Saturday Review, 135
Schenectady, N. Y., 13
Scribner's, 14
Selected Poems, 22
Seven Arts Magazine, 21
Shaftsbury, Vermont, 77
Shakespeare, William, 17
Shelley, P. B., 71
"Ships," 114
Shirley, James, 125
Sidney, Philip, 62
Silver Lake, New Hampshire, 138, 144
Sloane, William, 85
Smythe, Ruth, 132, 133, 145, 146, 150, 151, 152
Snow, Wilbert, 10, 65
"Song of the Wave," 17
Spender, Stephen, 128
Squires, J. C., 130, 140
Stark Family, 128

Steep Acres, 36
Steeple Bush, 23
Stephens, James, 73
"Stopping by Woods on a Snowy Evening," 57, 118
Stuart, Jessie, 96
Swedenborgian, 16, 43, 85
Swinburne, Algeron, 38
Swinger of Birches, A, 135

Taylor, Alexander, 121, 122, 127
Thomas, Edward, 20
Thompson, Dorothy, 55
Trails, 13, 146
Truman, Harry, 145, 147
Tufts College, 31, 34, 44, 54
Turner, Nancy Byrd, 51

Union College, 117
United States Senate, 12
Universalism, 85
Untermeyer, Louis, 12, 30, 74, 107, 127

Van Doran, Irita, 139
Van Doren, Mark, 133

Wallace, Henry, 97
Warren, Earl, 145, 147
Washington, D. C., 92, 93
Washington *Post*, 93
Webster, Daniel, 107
West-Running Brook, 22
Weygandt, Cornelius, 135
Wheelwright, John, 75
Whitman, Walt, 91, 144
Whittier, John Greenleaf, 138
Widener Library, 27
Wilcox, Ella Wheeler, 125
Williams, William Carlos, 139
Winslow, Ann, 40
"Witch of Coos," 117
Witness Tree, A, 23
Wylie, Philip, 133, 147

Yeats, William Butler, 128
Young Men's Hebrew Association, 142
Young, Stark, 21, 128